WAKING UP

8 QUESTIONS

That Will Shift Your Life

(Or Help You Do Nothing)

VINCE CORSARO

Waking Up: 8 Questions That Will Shift Your Life (Or Help You Do Nothing)

Copyright © 2019 Vince Corsaro

Distributed by Lulu Press, Morrison, North Carolina

ISBN: 978-0-359-82964-4

Contents

Preface: The Year My Life Went off the Rails

In 2004 my life looked good. I had been continuously employed and married for about 25 years. I had been a successful CEO with hundreds of employees and was about to move to the senior management team of a large national organization engaged with millions of people.

I had worked hard to get there. I had done it by "the book" which to me were the rules set by the conventional narrative of the late 70's and 80's. In that narrative the right path in life was to go to school, get a career, get married, work hard, get promoted, have kids, raise them, and sail off into the sunset.

So how was it possible that just over a year later my world was a f***ing mess?!? Everything I had put on the plate of my life had been fully scraped clean.

First my marriage ended. We had been friends in high school, connected in college, and it had felt right to venture into the big scary world together when we married at 21 years old. Over the years we had grown in different ways. I hold a "no-fault" view when relationships end and think we both realized that we didn't have what the other needed.

Then I lost my job. Perhaps I had stepped into a role that was beyond my capacity at the time. It was a humiliating and humbling fall. If I look in the rearview mirror though, there were a few warning signs that might have let me know that things weren't all okay.

> *"You better get on board with us if you want to keep your position," a colleague had said to me in the weeks leading up to the final and fateful conversation.*

> *"Pick your battles, Vince. Isn't it more important to live to fight another day?"*

It was not just the fact I lost my job that burned, it was also the way in which it was delivered. It was a phone call that came in while I was on the road just after completing an all-day workshop.

> *"Several members of the executive cabinet are being let go. I appreciate you keeping it a quiet affair. There is really no need for you to come back to the office. Your Assistant will pack things up and ship to you."*

In the moment, I felt betrayed. And, betrayal is an ugly thing. It felt terrible. Violating. An injustice inflicted. I felt victimized. I felt as if I had been made the villain. The scapegoat.

The third blow was that my youngest daughter had just headed off to college. When I delivered her to school on the other side of the country, I felt sad. We had spent a fair amount of time doing life together and traveling in the year since her Mom and I had separated. I also felt sorry for my older daughter who was already away for college and had the "perfect little family" ideal tossed out.

The final blow to my carefully constructed 'normal' life was that I began to acknowledge that I was gay. It wasn't new information to me and had been brewing for many years, but the conventional narrative of the 70's and 80's did not include being openly gay. Any friends in those early years who came out were rarely seen again, and I had chosen a different path, the road *more* traveled.

So, all that adds up to a plate scraped clean.

I was 47 years old, unemployed, my divorce had been final for eight months, and I was living alone in a month-to-month rental condo unsure of who I was or who I wanted to be.

This was an entirely new and humbling place for me.   To put it mildly, I felt lost.

I was upset and ashamed about being single. It was not what I expected and not part of the conventional narrative. I was unsettled yet thankful that my condo was decent and felt more stable than living in my Volkswagen van. But I had no idea what I was going to do with myself.

My life was at a critical transition point. I knew inside that I had made all kinds of mistakes, judgment errors, and had paid attention to many of the wrong things. I also knew that I never woke up in the morning thinking "How can I screw up today?" Each day had run in to the next and it all added up to 25 years of adulthood. But, I still had a sense that I had been asleep. Perhaps it was time to wake up.

The problem with living by any conventional narrative, like I had done, is that it is mostly unconscious. Asleep. "Follow the script" required little creative or intentionally conscious thought. By outside appearances, it seemed to work for me. In the end, it all finally collapsed.

So began my deeper inquiry into what I wanted and what I would make of my life. I had a lot of questions swirling around in my head. I also began to realize that "waking up" isn't a once done kind of thing. It's an ongoing process. Waking up is something we can choose to do daily. You might believe this too.

There was no good-bye party and I had no gold watch on my wrist. Instead I sat down to read William Bridges' book on "*Managing Transitions*" to see what I might be ready to learn.

I appreciated Bridges' idea that I needed to let go of all that had happened and spend some time in what he calls the "neutral zone", not making any long-term commitments, testing possibilities, seeing what maybe couldn't be seen before.

Bridges' point is that the more we invest in the neutral zone, the better equipped we are to create a new beginning. It made sense to me.

To help clear my head, I kayaked with some friends around Vancouver Island, took a long walk in the Scottish Highlands, and traveled with a colleague to the outback of Ghana to look at a possible eco-tourism project. Next, I completed a coaching certification and a series of process facilitation courses.

A friend once told me that what I do is help people untangle the knots in their heads. So, I knew I needed to untangle a bit. I needed to take a step back and use some good curious questions to shift and connect with myself in a whole new way.

So, I'll share some of those questions and serve them up in a way that might help you do the same in whatever circumstances you find yourself. Perhaps you will see yourself in some of the conversations I share. These are all real people with real stories. (In fact, these might be conversations I've had with YOU and you might be a bit anxious thinking "What is Vince going to expose here?!?")

My belief is that as we understand and connect with ourselves, we are better able to understand and connect with others. And, understanding starts with the willingness to shift into a place of curious wonder and the courage to learn new ways of knowing, and new ways of living.

But how do you "wonder"? To me, the wondering process requires doing nothing. Literally. I'm talking about sitting on the beach staring out at the water kind of nothing. We'll dig into this idea as we go and perhaps you will discover how doing nothing, or nothing differently, can produce a boost of energy and satisfaction in your life.

When I looked at what had happened in my life, what I made it all mean, how I felt, and what I wanted, I came up with a commitment to a way of living that embraces who I am and who I want to be. I am going to show you over the next few hours how to find such a commitment to guide your own life.

> *My commitment is to be a man of curiosity, with a spirit of adventure and creativity.*

That is who I am **to be.** What I aim to <u>do</u> is:

> *Live a life of good self-care and connect in authentic relationship with myself, and with others as they connect with themselves.*

In later chapters I will unpack how I got there.

My guess is you wouldn't be here if there wasn't something in your life to unpack. My guess is all of us have some good questions to ponder. Let's both ask and answer some together.

Today I am enjoying 13 years since crafting a solo practice in the area of executive leadership development and personal growth. I have a unique flavor in the way I approach the work and have benefited greatly from an eclectic mix of authors and friends in the field including Gaye Hendricks, Jim Warner, Kaley Warner Klemp, Dave Phillips, Richard Rohr, Rob Bell, Patrick Lencioni, Simon Sinek, Brene' Brown, Jim Dettmer, George Kinder, Dan Baker and a few others. At the end of the book I'll give you some "Reading and Resources". Back in the day a respected colleague said **"You Must Read to Lead**!" I believe that, and maybe you do too.

I have a set of conscious commitments that guide my life and enjoy a global circle of friends and associates. My life is rich and full, with plenty of ups and downs, adventures and curiosities. My hope is to simply make the world a friendlier place where everyone enjoys a sense of love and belonging with themselves and their tribe big or small.

Onward!

Vince
Palm Springs, California
www.vincecorsaro.com

Part I

Why Ask Questions Anyway?

My career was on a fast track and we had moved from Southern California so I could become a CEO in Boulder, Colorado. I was 35 and eager to make my mark. Coming from a successful run as a local operating executive, I was frankly full of myself. I knew what to do and, in my enthusiasm, expected everyone to be quite ready to hear what I had to say and march to my command. Perhaps.

Within a few weeks, I noticed that while people were happy to talk with me, they really weren't all that interested in changing anything. They were committed to the way they had always done things.

"But, where do I get to leave my mark?" I began to lament to myself. "These people are stuck in an old mindset, they have no plan, they are entrenched, and all the power is being held by the wrong people. Can't they see it?" I became more and more critical. Disillusioned.

At about 90-days in, the Human Resources Manager, who was a couple years younger than me and smart as a whip, came into my office and closed the door. What follows that moment when an HR Manager closes the door is rarely good. So, I braced myself.

"You know Vince" she said, "We somehow managed to survive for almost a hundred years before you got here. From your questions and how you are moving about, it sounds like you don't think we've ever done anything right. You might get a better response if you showed up with a little more curiosity."

Hmm, I thought. Sometimes a 2x4 upside the head hurts.

The Reason Most Questions Kill Curiosity

Many leaders are good producers, good problem solvers, good at fixing things and getting things done. But, they are lousy question askers. They know how to answer questions, which often has gotten them promoted. Those good at answering questions are not necessarily good at asking them. I was one of them!

In my role as CEO I had been coming from a place of criticism. I saw problems with the way things were being done. I was digging in to clarify and confirm that my criticisms were correct and that things needed to change. Instead of appreciating what was going right, I had been on a hunt to verify what was wrong. And, the troops were pushing back against me, defending themselves, and drawing the battle lines. Yikes!

The reason most questions kill curiosity is that too often the question invites defensiveness, deflection, or shame. "Why did you do that?" "Who is to blame for this?" "What is the matter with you?"

When we are defending ourselves, we are not learning.

When we are deflecting, we are not taking responsibility for the results in our life.

When we are mired in shame, we are protecting our identity.

Not ideal.

My experience is that good curious questions are incredibly rare in most conversations. I sense that they are rare because, when a good, curious, thought-provoking question does land, it's like a shot of oxygen in the room. People stop. Things get quiet. People breathe. Almost always, someone says, "Now, that's a good question." I love it when a question makes everyone stop.

How to ask good questions is something we must learn.

What's A Good Question?

Now, that's a good question!

A good question helps me separate the facts in any situation from all the stories I might make up about those facts. A good question might also help uncover the emotions in play. Some good questions bring clarity. Almost always, a good question helps me shift into curiosity. Let's look at what makes a good, curious, thought-provoking question.

A Good Question Has At Least One of Four Qualities

Invites Story and Meaning

Create understanding of why this issue is important. Opens the possibility to opposite stories, old stories, un-founded stories.

Confirms Data

Gives a factual basis to the conversation, issue, or dynamic. Checks for accuracy. Filters out assumptions, theoretical possibilities, and dramatic flair.

Clarifies Deeper Wants

Gets to the heart of the matter. Gives guidance to options and future actions. Describes a desired future and recognizes that the desired future may not occur.

Discovers Emotional Undercurrent

Welcomes emotional experience and expression. Accepts and allows as opposed to defend or deny. Opens the doorway to authentic desire.

A good question helps remind you that whatever is going on today is just part of the much bigger story of your life. A good question helps *shift your altitude* to the horizon view, a global or lifetime view, or the 12- inch shift from the thoughts in your head to the passion in your heart. When you shift, the door opens to make sense of whatever is going on in your life today in a more grounded and curious way. A new perspective, perhaps. A good question often helps shift you from focusing on the data of your life to discovering the meaning of your life.

So, let's go a little deeper.

Quality 1: A Good Question Confirms the Data

Data is important. A good question will confirm that there is a factual basis to the conversation. Sometimes, just focusing on the data, as in, "what really happened here?" is all that it takes to get to the root of the matter.

And there is typically very little data involved in any singular scene! So, I challenge myself to get curious about just three specific data points that might be coming into play in the moment.

- I had been continuously employed for 26 years and was let go.
- My divorce was finalized.
- My youngest had left for college.

But what do you really learn from the facts? Not much, frankly. They might give some context to the conversation, but don't really create a sense of understanding, significance, or urgency. That comes next.

Quality 2: A Good Question Invites Story and Meaning

While data is important to contextualize a moment, a good question is often NOT one that seeks to **probe** for data. Questions probing for more data often come from my desire to build a case for my solution for your life. I just need a few more facts to confirm my solution. So, I NEVER (okay, rarely) ask questions of data. I trust you to give me the data that is important to you. Data is a lot like cocktail party chitchat. And, I don't really like cocktail parties.

What I DO like is to learn about you.

What makes you tick?

What gets your heart pumping?

What do you look forward to and what do you f***ing dread?

 I want to know what you are making your life mean. So, my (better) questions almost always open a door for you to share some of your story. And, I'm happy to share some of my story as well.

A big idea here is that stories are mostly fiction. Your story is what you make all the data in your life mean. As author and awesome speaker **Brene' Brown** says, "Stories are data with a soul." So, with whatever data you might choose to give me, I can invite you to share some story about it.

- You told me you are a new dad. What was most surprising about your ten-month journey?
- You told me you are a weight lifter. What are you hoping to achieve? What are you learning about yourself as you gain strength and stature?
- You told me that there is twelve inches of new powder. How do you feel about that? What is it you want to have happen today?
- You told me you went to Israel last summer. What was gratifying or upsetting?

The fun part of a good story question is that you get to listen to the answer. You create a connection through shared story. Maybe you get to see a little bit of your own story in others and recognize that your story is simply your story! Your thoughts are yours, and anything you might believe to be true is simply, what you might believe to be true.

The bottom line: We make up stories ALL THE TIME. And, that means we can also MAKE UP A DIFFERENT STORY!

Here is an internal dialogue a client shared. He was having some tension in his relationship and came to realize how much of the tension was being driven by the stories he was creating.

> *She said: "I shouldn't have to tell you how to express love to me. You should just know... naturally."*
>
> *What he heard: "I'm a screw-up. I don't know how to love well."*
>
> *Then he remembered: "I get to choose how her statements land for me. Just because she says something is true about me doesn't make it true."*
>
> *He re-framed his thoughts: "Ah. Perhaps she struggles expressing clear wants. **What's my part in this? What can I own?"***

Then he explored: "Well, I can listen intently and affirm her when she does express a want. I can offer her optional choices from time to time and learn about her wants. I can experiment with different kinds of love expressions and see what lands as love for her... time, touch, service, gifts, and words... I could find a time when the tension is low and invite her to tell me some stories about when she has felt loved. When her wants were heard. And, I can listen and learn."

Making the shift from *"I don't love well"* to *"I can listen and learn how to take full responsibility for my part in this relationship"* isn't easy. It takes guts. And, it's the power in recognizing how story is just story.

Here is another example of a real-life dialogue that helped shed light on the way what you say really has little bearing on what I hear. It so clearly showed me how whatever is going on in this current moment is over-shadowed by all the previous moments of my life.

And then he told me about a spat with his wife the night before. They were visiting one of his construction job sites.

She said: "Wouldn't it look better to extend the awning over this whole section?"

He said: "Don't you know I've been working on this design for months and that it is way too late in the process for changes like that?"

And on and on. The "He Said/She Said" game. Everyone had retreated into their corners before it was over.

So, I asked, **"What did you make her comment mean?"**

"Good question. I'll have to write that down."

"Well? It sounds like her comment landed in your universe as something more than just her comment. **What did it mean to you? What was the message you received?"**

"That I've fallen short. Didn't do it right. That I never do things right."

"Wow. She didn't say all that. **Whose voice was it you heard?"**

Silence. "It was my dad. I could never do anything right in his eyes."

"Sounds like you emptied your truck at the wrong dump, huh?"

The fascinating thing about stories is that we often get the characters mixed up. You say something that becomes what my dad used to say to me and suddenly I'm in an emotional swirl and you've become my dad. Yikes!

I had my own story (or a few!) and it was sometimes a great question asked by a friend that allowed me to see it. One of my stories was that being a gay man would hurt my career.

We were in a nice restaurant in San Francisco. He was a CEO/client and a good guy. I had just shared with him that I was coming out gay.

> *"So, how has that impacted your work?" he asked with marked curiosity.*
>
> *"Well, it hasn't hurt it yet," I started.*
>
> *But then, I stopped. I took a breath, and realized that my lifetime belief that "being gay would be a disaster" was driving my response. In a moment, I began to question that longheld belief and begin the process of embracing a new belief. I stumbled for the next words.*
>
> *My voice quivered a bit. I felt nervous "In my work it has been awesome. People have gravitated to the authenticity of it. Nothing but complete acceptance and a strengthening of my practice. In other relationships, not so much."*

"I thought so. I was surprised that wasn't your first answer. And, I get it. You've carried another story for a long time."

Quality 3: A Good Question Uncovers the Emotional Undercurrent

A good question welcomes the emotional experience. And whether the emotional experience is a feeling or a bodily sensation, a good question accepts and allows it rather than forcing you to defend or deny it.

Emotions simply are. In my thinking, there is no such thing as a positive or negative emotion. "I feel sad." "I feel angry." "I feel afraid." "I feel joyful." As you learn to experience your emotions, you become more connected to the truth of who you are in that moment. And, you can be conscious in your choice of how to respond in that emotion. Being angry is not a bad thing. Hitting someone over the head with a baseball bat is. Emotions are like waves that wash over us on the shoreline. They come in and they go out.

I love the line in the Chevy Chase movie, "Man of the House" where his character's new friend George welcomes him "to the tribe of emotionally constipated men." You see, our culture works hard at eliminating emotion from our lives.

"Boys don't cry"
(Read: The emotion of sadness is not acceptable)
"Girls are always polite"

(Read: The emotion of anger is not acceptable)
"There is no place for emotion in the workplace"
(Read: Work is full of dead people)

I was one of these men so it was only in the late 90's that I began a quest to connect with my emotions. Like many, I had learned early on how to suppress, repress, ignore, deny, defend, or otherwise plug up the valves of my emotional experience. I was "constipated". In one of my early experiences I attended a men's conference aimed at helping us "get in touch" with our emotions. Since men are generally simple beings at heart, the leaders wisely only gave us four choices - mad, sad, bad or glad. We called them "The Big Four" and learned to also know them as anger, sadness, fear, and joy respectively.

As I've come to learn, the Big Four are really buckets that hold a whole litany of emotions. Tender, soft, down, depressed, hurt, and tearful all point to sadness. Frustrated, irritated, mad, and upset all point to anger. Anxious, worried, bad, exposed, vulnerable and guilty point to fear. And finally, compassionate, happy, alive, grateful, and grounded tend to point toward joy.

Some words we use to describe feelings really are more the absence of any feeling at all or the confusing jumble of conflicting emotions. These might be overwhelmed, numb, and ashamed. When these come up, there is always room for the question, "When I judge that I am overwhelmed, am I feeling mad, sad, bad, or glad?"

Shifting from the story of your life to how you feel about that story is a simple step that can be encouraged by the good question,

"When I think about all that, how do I feel?"

And, when you are feeling, just feel! Meet yourself in that emotion and allow it. Notice it. The cool thing here is that your body can give you some great information! Emotional <u>response</u> almost always comes with a physical sensation that you can experience if you are open to it. Where is it showing up in your body? Is there a tightness or softness somewhere? Are tears wanting to flow? And then, you can become curious and wonder about what the message might be from the sensation. What deeper truth might the emotion be pointing to?

In pursuing the connection to my emotional experience, it was helpful for me to ask, "How do I feel?" regularly. And, to keep it simple, I only used the four primary emotions. I became adept at tying emotion to whatever I was feeling in my body. I believed myself when I would think, "Oh, my shoulders are tight, I must be mad." Or, "that sinking feeling in my gut combined with tears is sadness. I feel sad."

And then a few years ago I was surfing at an unfamiliar break- Pacific Beach in San Diego- and while paddling into a wave became concerned that it was too big and that I didn't have the capability to ride it well. By the time I made the decision to pull back I was too far in and ended up getting "sucked over the falls" and slammed on to the shallow sandy bottom. I knew immediately that things weren't right and managed to get myself out of the water. I was stunned and disoriented but not enough to warrant medical attention on the spot. After suffering in pain for a week or so, I had x-rays taken and found that there were two compression fractures in my lower back. And, I've never been the same.

I went to physical therapy and chiropractic. Folks suggested all kinds of supplements and pills. I did exercises and stretches. I hydrated well. But if stress is going to show up in my body, it goes straight to my back. And it's a pain.

But sometimes, the sensation just wants to be allowed as a sensation. Maybe it's more important to just feel and let go of trying to attach any meaning to the feeling.

The Body Therapist was exploring some painful areas in my lower back. At one brutally painful spot he stopped and asked, "So what was going on in your life when this happened?"

"How should I know!?" was my initial response. But then I got quiet with the question. "Well, I was actually in a pretty good spot. Things were going well at home and at work. It was a surfing accident."

"An accident?! Hmm." He smirked.

"What!?" I cried as he dug a little deeper.

"Is there more to the story?" he asked.

"Well, the story is more what followed the accident. The pain I have lived with. The capacity lost. I can't stand up when I get out of a chair. It's a real pain."

"I get it. But let's try this. Let's forget all those words for a moment. Forget how and when it

happened. Let's just focus on the pain in your back and what it feels like. Is it hot? What color might represent the pain? Where does the sensation start? Where does it end?"

As he slowly brought all my awareness to the pain something happened. The pain left. It subsided.

"Okay, what kind of voodoo are you performing?" I cried.

What he suggested was that I just allow the sensation I was having to simply be a sensation and focus on it that way. In a sense, he said, "Let go of all the story you make up about the sensation and just experience it as a sensation." It has been incredibly helpful to me. Instead of getting wrapped up in any kind of made-up story, I can just simply notice my back feeling tight or any number of other sensations that I feel regularly. When I focus on them as a sensation, they tend to abate.

Quality 4: A good question helps clarify a deeper want.

What is it you really want? And if you had that, what would you really have? Are you willing to let go of your want, recognizing that you don't always get what you want? And, the list goes on.

Asking yourself good questions can get to the heart of the matter.

Any way you slice it, every step you take is a choice. No matter how you got here, no matter how f***ing messed up your world has been, the next step is a choice. No doubt you can be bound to old beliefs and old stories and justify your circumstances, but you can also embrace your deeper desires and begin to take steps toward that desire.

But that means you must get clear on your desire. What it is you want. And, that's when the work starts.

In the week before the 2010 California Governor's election, a campaign typified by particularly bruising negative attacks, both candidates for governor were appearing together and asked if they would take down their negative ads.

Jerry Brown, the former governor who was ultimately elected said, "If Meg wants to do that, I'll be glad to do that."

And Meg said, "I will take down any ads that could be even remotely construed as a personal attack, but I don't think we can take down ads that talk about where Governor Brown stands on the issues."

So, who gets the gold star for clear communication?

Sadly, not re-elected Jerry. While Meg got booed for her remark, Jerry was lauded with praise. But what did he really say? Look carefully.

He said nothing!

He played a classic move of political non-speak. He could have said, "I want to take down the negative ads." Or better yet, "I will take down all negative ads. Meg, will you agree to that?" But he didn't say that. He said, "If Meg wants to..."

So, good questions invite you to speak clearly what it is you want in your life. Not what you don't want. Not what you want for others. And, when you notice yourself framing a thought about what you don't want... just make a shift. Get curious and ask yourself, "Well, if I don't want that, what is it that I DO want?"

And remember, a want is simply your want. Recognize that you don't always get what you want!

It is not easy to recognize what you truly want. A big part of my work is helping folks get clear on that. I remember a session with a popular Hollywood celebrity. It took a bit of digging to get there but she eventually got to a deeper want.

> *"No one ever calls me to just have coffee, or to do the things that friends do. We don't get invited to informal dinners, to just hang out. No one just stops by. Everything is fabulous and formal or nothing at all. Sometimes I feel like the only reason anyone wants to be with me is to get something from me. I think people just assume I'm busy. It's exhausting."*

> *I said. "How would you like it to be? What is it you are wanting?"*

> *"I'd like to have people who feel comfortable just hanging out. No agendas. People who know I'll say 'yes' if it is possible. People who know that if I say*

'no' it's a real no, meaning I've already got something booked."

"So, what you really want are friends who are authentic with you."

"Not just authentic, but who are okay with me saying no three times without it counting against me!"

I got quiet. You see, I get in this same pickle. My schedule is erratic, unstructured, and unpredictable. I can be anywhere or nowhere anytime. I fall off the radar screen regularly and rarely get casual invitations from friends. I had no solution to offer. Which is perfect, because I'm in the business of helping people find their own solutions. So, back to it, Vince.

"I wonder how you might be creating the very results you're complaining about?"

"Are you playing one of your mind tricks on me?"

"Well, perhaps. And, perhaps I'm playing it on both of us. But, really, what are the things you do that create the exact results you're getting?"

"Let's see. I tend to only talk about the projects I'm on, or the places I've been lately. I rarely talk about the mundane and normal things in life. I don't tend to talk about the supermarket having a special on tomatoes this week." She gazed off in the distance a bit.

"So, what do you think others make that mean?"

"I suppose it makes me seem above the mundane. Maybe others are intimidated to talk about tomatoes when I've just gotten back from a month-long location shoot on the Italian Riviera. Maybe I put people off a bit."

"Keep going," I prodded.

"Do I really want to talk about tomatoes?"

My sense was that there was a part of her that precisely wanted to talk about the mundane and normal things of life, like tomatoes at the local market. I also sensed there was another part of her that had absolutely no interest in talking about tomatoes and only wanted to talk about the exciting and interesting bits. Perhaps there was a path...

"It sounds like we have competing voices here. On the one side we have a voice going... Be normal! Enjoy and appreciate the mundane and simple life! It's about connection, not about amazement! You are okay when you are ordinary!"

"And on the other side?"

"The other voice says...you have to shine. You must entertain! Everyone expects you to be interesting! They will leave you in the dust if you're not!"☐

I could tell something was landing for her. She fell silent.

"That's exactly what my dad used to say to me." And then, tears. *"My Dad always wanted me to perform. He'd have me sing at family events. He only seemed to notice me if I was performing. I think he was afraid I would disappear or be a nobody if I didn't entertain well."*

"So, it sounds like you keep performing even when the cameras are off. Tell me what the tears have to say right now."

"My tears like the other voice. My whole body just wants to let down my guard. To just be normal, ordinary, mundane. To just connect. I can breathe when I think about that."

"Okay. What would that look like?" I asked.

"Well, maybe I can be more conscious of what I share and engage with others about. Maybe I can talk about tomatoes now and then. And, not how fabulous my homegrown crop is. You know what I mean. Just, ask others about the simple pleasures of their lives. Share the ordinary. It doesn't need to be fabulous."

"And if you did that, what might you get?"

"Well, I think it would just be more authentic. I want authenticity in my life. And, frankly, that's worth it, regardless if anyone ever calls me for coffee."

After Some Good Questions: Make One Small Commitment

While good questions might uncover the facts, stories, feelings, and wants, that's not the end of the story. A good question moves us toward action. And, not just any old action, but purposeful and conscious action. We'll explore this much further later but I want to stop here and play with the idea of small commitments.

For me, getting clarity on what I wanted in life was not an easy task. Years working in the social sector had left me with a lost sense of personal identity. I had been living the mission of my work for so long that it had become my mission. My sense of personal purpose was muddy at best. At worst I had no clue.

So, as I started to become clear in what I wanted my life to be, I knew I needed to start small. And, I got very small. I knew I wanted to take responsibility for all parts of my life including disciplines around daily living. So, I committed to a cleaned-up living space every day and to know what I wanted for dinner every night. Just that.

I share this commitment with groups now and then and love the responses.

"Well, what I want for dinner is whatever my wife is makin' for dinner," said the guy in Houston with a lovely southern drawl.

"I haven't made a bed in years. Don't you have staff for that?"

"Why bother saying what I want for dinner when we go out? I'll just get over-ruled."

"Really, Vince. That's the best commitment you could come up with?"

And, it served me well. Because there is something powerful in taking action toward a stated want. It means you have given thought to your life. It's a daily reminder that you can say what you want, stay true to your commitments, and live to tell about it! It helps us learn that sometimes you don't get what you want, but it is still your want. And, starting with small wants often paves the way to discover your bigger wants and greater purposes.

Recently, I had a conversation with myself reflecting on relationships with my siblings. As it turns out, none of my siblings enjoy travel or have an interest at this stage of life in exploring the bigger world. I've complained about this to myself before and in a moment of clarity I said, "I want some siblings that could meet me in far flung places in the world!" And, something happened. By clarifying my want, I was able to release it as simply a want. And, I know that I don't always get what I want.

Summary: Good Questions

Where do you see an opportunity to create a new set of facts in your life?

What are the stories you are making up about you?

When you think about all that, how do you feel?

What is it you want? For you? Today? In life?

And then what is the One Small Commitment you can make right now to guide your steps in getting what you want in your life?

BEFORE YOU GO ANY FURTHER:
WANTS AND RISKS

Right now, I invite you to give some thought to your life with some good questions. We will revisit this life audit later in the book and unpack it a bit more. You can also look ahead and see my Playbook in Part 3, but that might be cheating. Write it out on another page or use this worksheet. Play with it. You may not be able to fill it all in.

As you do this, give yourself a kudo for articulating what you want in your life and the positive commitments you are making to guide your steps. All good! Put these on the wall. Shout it from the mountaintops. You are doing the work of becoming you.

And, maybe you've done all this before. But guess what! The picture of you yesterday is not the picture of you today. Perhaps, this time is simply an opportunity to re-focus your own binoculars. What is the new information in your life since you last thought about your wants and commitments? Are your commitments continuing to serve you in ways that are satisfying, rich, and full?

If so, great! Keep it up.

Waking Up: The First Look in the Mirror

What are some of the facts in your life right now? What could a video camera record about your actions, activities and relationships?	
And, what does all that mean to you? Where are you most satisfied? Least Satisfied? Where are you getting things done and where are you stuck? If you were writing the fictional story of your life, what would be high points? The low points?	
When you think about all that, how do you feel? What emotions come up as you reflect upon your whole life?	
As you get clear on all the meaning you create and the emotions you feel, what is it you really want? Not so much a "to do" as an end state you aspire to?	
If that is what you want, what is one small commitment you could make to yourself that might guide your action steps? Not a single action step but a path or a way of living?	

And, if you see an opportunity for improvement or a place where you see yourself stuck, it might be worthwhile to unpack it a bit more. But before you do, let's consider the risks of even looking at your life. Because, it just might be too risky. Listen in:

> *"I really want to make some changes," she said. "I can't keep going on like this."*

> *"Okay. Let's talk about that. Is this the right time to make some changes?" I asked.*

> *"Ha! My life is like a house of cards. Everything is barely balancing against everything else. My husband is unhappy but not too unhappy. The kids are doing just okay, not great. My boss knows that I know too much to fire me."*

> *"That sounds pretty complicated. What might be the risks of taking a look at all that?"*

> *"Honestly, I don't know that I can. I want things to be different. Better. But really, what if I discovered that it's me that is unhappy with him? What if I decide that it's not working? What would I do then?"*

> *"You'd have some tough choices to make. That's a risk. You might discover that the relationship isn't working for you."*

> *"Vince, I appreciate you asking about whether it's the right time. Because, it's not. I just can't take the risk of messing with the house of cards."*

"Congratulations. You just set a boundary in your life. Let's unpack that a bit."

The Big Idea here is that we are managing risk all the time: the risk of failure, risk of exposure, risk of unwanted change, risk of being vulnerable, risk of success or things getting too good. We'll talk more about the risk of actual change later, but for now it is important to assess the risk of even engaging in the inquiry. To even explore an issue must mean something to you or you would have likely explored and resolved it long ago. It might peel a scab off an old wound.

Assessing risk is something you do in business all the time. "Risk/Benefit Analysis" likely comes naturally to you in any number of work settings. And, the same idea applies to your life. What is the risk of looking at your life? What is the possible benefit of doing so? Are you willing to take the risk?

Another way to approach the idea of risk is to look at what keeps you right where you are. Is your life a house of cards that can't take the pressure of even looking? Is something that you are complaining about actually protecting you from some greater risk?

When you assess the risk of even exploring your life and decide the answer is "no", what happens next? You stop complaining. You have looked at the risks and possible benefits and made a conscious choice to stay the course, **do**

nothing different, and not explore the issue further. You've set a boundary of what is yours and what is not yours at this time. No more energy drain thinking about thinking about it! Move on. Live.

While this is a real conversation, I've heard variations on this one from almost everyone in my life. What about you?

> *"I need to eat better. I need to drop some weight. I'm a glutton at night. Anything in the house is fair game."*

> *"Wow. Sounds like you know how to beat yourself up. Do you want to explore this?"*

> *"Sure, so we can find more ways to beat myself up?"*

> *"I hope not. What is it you think you want?"*

> *"To be fit, dammit!"*

> *"Okay. let's say you want to be fit. What might you have to let go of to be fit?"*

> *"Look. I know it's trendy and popular to eat super healthy food. All the right proteins, dark green leafy whatever, omega 47 foods that I can't pronounce. I don't want to give up the way I eat and drink and I don't want to even think about it!"*

"Okay. What would happen if you didn't give that up?"

"I'll turn in to a beer-gutted pudge and die an early death!"

"Maybe. It sounds to me that even exploring the idea of how you eat and drink would bring the risk of a boring or unsatisfying life that no one would want to live."

"Go on."

"What if you just said no to even thinking about it? What if you allowed yourself to not give up the foods and drinks you like?"

"Ha! I'm paying you for this?"

"Stick with me. I'm inviting you to simply own it as a way of living that you are not wanting to explore. It's too risky. It sounds to me like you are clear on what you are committed to."

"Right! I'm committed to eating and drinking whatever I want!"

"Perfect. Let's check in later and see how it works out for you."

What happened here? I invited him to do nothing different in his life. And, to quit all the internal flogging he was doing to himself. Let it go! Roll the tape forward six months. We're at an offsite and just finished a water ski run after a day of strategic conversations. He was popping a beer and looked at me with a knowing smile:

> *"Remember Vince! I am committed to eating and drinking whatever I want!"*

> *"Got it! How's that working out for you?"*

> *"Ha! I've dropped twenty pounds and feel stronger than I have felt in years."*

> *"Tell me more."*

> *"Look, you played your voodoo on me and it worked. By letting go of all the beat-the-shit-out-of-myself I started being more conscious about whether I really wanted that bag of Oreos before bed. More often, there was something else going on that was driving me in that moment. We also stopped buying Oreos."*

So, by choosing to say no to the risk of exploring what might be a dissatisfying life focused on quinoa and kale he instead focused on what he really wanted and allowed himself to make a more conscious choice in each moment. More on this idea of "doing nothing" as we go.

Back to the idea of the risk of exploring your life. What if the answer is "Yes?" And, I mean a full-body heart-mind-soul in alignment "Yes! I am willing to take the risk in order to gain the possible benefits!" This opens the door for you to enter an inquiry with your eyes open. Fully conscious and aware that there may be some challenging and vulnerable moments ahead. Your fears are in front of you. And what happens when you shine a light on fear? It often dissipates. Becomes less powerful. So, assessing risks and benefits almost always begins the process of clearing away the underbrush to get to the real issues.

Up until the moment that my life was scraped clean, I was in a "no" position in this regard. I could not afford the risk of really looking at myself. I was living in the house of cards my client referred to earlier. For me, the risk didn't change until external forces and circumstances changed. So, sometimes (actually, much of the time), external forces bring us to a place where risk is inherently reduced and benefit is almost assured. Doing nothing different becomes a very limited option. It might be different for you.

It's also helpful when thinking about the risk of exploring your life to consider that you may have some longheld beliefs that are in play. We'll talk about this much more later, but for now, it's a good idea to consider what is it you believe about life change? What do you believe about your ability to step into a place of curiosity and wonder? And then, consider that beliefs are something that you can choose to embrace or release. So, what beliefs might you want to put "on hold" for a time of exploration?

Before You Start Ask Yourself....

- Have you fully accepted where your life is a f*** mess?
- Where do you see an opportunity for growth in your life?
- What are the risks associated with even looking at this area of your life?
- What long-held beliefs might come into play? What beliefs might want to be put on hold as you explore this?
- Why have you not looked at it before now?
- How does it serve you to not look at your life?
- How might you benefit from looking at your life?
- Are you willing to take the risk of looking in order to possibly gain the benefits of doing so?
- And if not, are you willing to let go of your right to complain about this area of your life?

PART 2

While we've danced around the idea of good questions and the risks of even asking them, let's start looking at the sequence. We start at the beginning with exploring the reality of what is happening or what has happened. We'll get to all eight questions, but for now we'll focus on the first four.

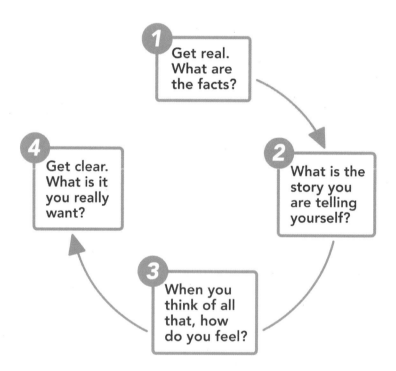

QUESTION ONE: Get Real. What are the facts?

We've all had an "it" moment. That moment when some new thing captures your attention. A new model car. A second glance by an attractive man or woman. The possibility of a new VP of Sales to replace the old guy. An old flame entering from 'stage right'. It really doesn't matter what "it" is.

It's a **new red shiny**.

And, suddenly! That new red shiny begins to represent a perfect future reality of your life as it was meant to be! A new beginning! A fresh start! Coffee in bed every morning. Beautiful sunsets. Off the chart sales. Prestige and Power. No more laundry. No more diapers. No more disappointing sales reports. Doesn't matter! The future has arrived and it's perfect! The new red shiny can wipe away years and years of un-expressed emotions, disappointments, shortfalls, neglect, guilt... all of it! Go! Jump! Take the leap and you will learn to fly!!!

And what about the old car? That piece of trash? Lousy mileage. 20 pounds overweight. Lazy and stuck in a rut of low production. Heading nowhere. At least, nowhere good. Or, worth going. Dump it. Who needs it? I've put up with it long enough. There is nothing new, red, or shiny there.

In fact, it's old, black, and tarnished. Dead end. Might as well go die a lonely death in a gutter in Central Park before living with that. I deserve better. In fact, it's *their* fault. They've caused me to be miserable. The new red shiny "gets me" and this old black tarnished thing... well... Whatever.

Sound familiar? Well, I've heard it many times in my years as an executive coach. And, I've said many of these things personally.

So, what to do?

It doesn't really matter which train you are riding; the questions are pretty much the same. Whether you're heading down the track to the perfect future reality or imagining the cliff at the end of the track of despair and worst possible outcome, the truth is that you are making up a story. And, we're damn good at making up stories.

So, when you catch yourself on either train, you do well to stop. Take a breath. Get real.   And, this starts with separating the FACT from the FICTION.

Ask yourself:

> What's really happening here?
> What might a video camera record?
> What would an observer see here?
> What are the triggering events?

Once you've assessed the risk of exploring the issue, start with the facts. Starting with a presentation of data ("just the facts") helps ground your inquiry because **facts are observable and quantifiable**. Facts are not feelings. Facts are not thoughts.

> *"The facts are we did a lousy job on that project!" the CEO proclaimed.*
>
> *"Really!" I said. "What actually happened?"*
>
> *"It doesn't matter what really happened. I think we did a lousy job and I think we could do better!" she shot back.*
>
> *"Ah. Sounds like you have a clear opinion about all that."*

So, what were the underlying facts behind this CEO's opinion?

The facts might have been:

1. They delivered the project to the customer thirty days later than the original agreement.
2. Engineering costs exceeded budget by 25%.
3. The senior VP spent four days with the project teams to unwind the critical path.

Those were the facts. Everything else was her opinion. And that's okay. Just don't call them facts. More good questions to uncover the facts might be:

- What has happened? Who? What? When? Where? How Many?
- Is there general agreement on the data by all parties?
- Are there differing versions of the facts?

The interesting thing is how few facts there really are driving the mental energy we commit to any topic or issue.

In September 2006, the facts were that I was unemployed, kids off at college, divorced and living in a rented condo.

Left alone as just facts, you really have no idea what any of that <u>meant to me.</u>

No matter what you are starting to unpack, I challenge you to come up with **three pertinent and distinct facts**. Because the facts are just facts. The fun starts when we delve into the stories, thoughts, beliefs, and assessments.

> *"It's excruciating to think about coming clean. I've been carrying this for so long, beating myself up for what I've done, feeling bad about the impact. I can't imagine unpacking it." he said.*

> *"I get it. You've been carrying this for a long time and it feels excruciating to think about unpacking it and coming clean. What's the real risk?" I asked.*

> *"Clearly that she'll throw me out. I'm a scumbag."*

> *"Got it. Your relationship might end. What else?"*

"I don't know. It seems like it might also be a relief to not carry it."

"Is that a risk, or a possible benefit?"

*"Ha! You got me. That would be a benefit. To me at least. **Would it be a benefit to her**?" he asked with curiosity.*

"Now, that's a great question."

Getting something off your chest, letting go of the remorse or guilt that you have carried around some issue or action can bring incredible relief. AND, it brings risk. Risk that the relationship might end. Risk that coming clean with what you've been carrying may result in harm or hurt. AND, it brings a significant benefit of possible renewal. The authentic ownership of an issue or action opens the door to the renewal of the relationship both with yourself and with the other person involved. But there's a catch.

The thing that has been carried for so long is new information for the other person. So, while there is relief on the one side, there can be all kinds of emotional responses on the other. They haven't been living with the remorse, guilt, and fear that have resulted from the facts that you've carried. So, your sense of relief can be viewed as a "dump and run." Some compassion is in order! And, this is true anytime you speak a courageous truth. At its best, coming clean creates compassion for ourselves and the other person while promoting authenticity in the relationship. At its worst, it becomes an emotional dumping ground and an escape from responsibility.

Question One In a Nutshell
Get Real. What are the Facts?

- So, the facts are...
- What has happened? Who? What? When? Where? How Many?
- Is there general agreement on the data by all parties?
- What are three factual bullet points that frame the issue?
- What are the most pertinent and important facts to know in order to assess?
- What could a video camera have recorded?
- What are the verifiable and objective metrics?
- Is there general agreement on the facts?
- What are the differing versions of the facts?
- What would be admissible as evidence in a crime case?
- Where is there disagreement on the facts?
- What are the specific behaviors observed?
- What was the specific time and place?
- What facts are missing? What facts need to be discovered?
- What are your agreements?

QUESTION TWO:
What is the story you are telling yourself?

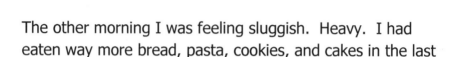

The other morning I was feeling sluggish. Heavy. I had eaten way more bread, pasta, cookies, and cakes in the last two weeks than anyone should.

When I'm feeling sluggish, I resist stepping on the scale. My commitment is to live at 190 +/- five pounds. The last time I had checked was an all-time high of 199. I don't ever want to see 200 so I simply stopped checking.

But that morning, something compelled me to step on to the scale and get ready for the inner barrage of criticism and justification. I didn't want to do it, but I knew I needed to. I needed to know that I had tipped 200. I needed to see the results of all that bad behavior. I needed to step on to the whipping post for some self-flagellation. Bad Vince!

I stepped on. 192? Can't be. Step off. Step back on. 192. Huh.

So, the truth is I think I'm a slug, glutton and undisciplined sloth for the way I've eaten my way through the last two weeks. But the data shows that I am seven pounds lighter.

What is the truth?

Is this a trick question?

No. Because the truth is that the message landing in my universe was "you're a slug, glutton, and undisciplined sloth." That's MY story. My truth. The FACT that I weighed seven pounds less than two weeks ago is un-important. The experience of my inner critical voice is my truth. That is the story I am telling myself.

Now, the truth is also that when the scale said 192, my mood shifted. I smiled. I felt less sluggish.

What I am learning is that much of what we call "truth" are really "beliefs." Things we believe to be true. I was believing that I was heavier, and my critical thoughts followed and chimed in.

And, that is the next step! Consider any good question that helps make sense of the data and discover your **thoughts and beliefs**. Dig deep. Go to the most critical stories you make up about you.

So, while these questions may help you get there, the big idea when engaging into the story is to find the most critical, dark, judgmental, complaining, blaming, victimizing, and vilifying stories possible. Brene Brown calls this your "shitty first draft."

Reflecting on my story in 2006, the self-flagellation (more on the "You Suck!" message later) was primarily around the shame and loss of the conventional narrative of 2.3 kids and a Volvo in the driveway. The harm I was creating for "kids from a broken home." The shame of having worked so long in the non-profit sector (read: "less than real work"). The cliché scenario of a rented condo just waiting for a convertible in the driveway. There were dark moments and I could go a week without having contact with any other human other than my therapist or my Friday morning coffee group. (More on the importance of a confidential peer group later).

And importantly, allowing the dark stories opened the possibility of an opposite story. It took a while to get there (and a year of anti-depressants), but eventually I did. In time, I was able to see a story of positive intent, of learning good judgment from bad experiences, and shifting from an immature view of the world to a more mature posture. Embracing the dark story opened my pathway to growth.

Sometimes when that new red shiny presents itself, it can become a sign from the universe, the divine, God, or however you describe that invisible force that you had nothing to do with but might be bringing you something good! You can write all kinds of story into it.

"Yes! It's not ME going for the new red shiny, it's the Universe opening a door! It's a spiritual awakening! I must follow God's leading in my life."

Another opportunity to stop. Take a breath. And, another breath.   And then, inquire within, how has God revealed Himself before? Is this consistent with His voice? What is

He thinking about your life and what you've made of it? If this new red shiny is good for you, is it good for all concerned? Are you only seeing the Universe playing on one path? If the divine is showing up in a critical, defensive, one-sided, never-been-this-way-before kind of way you might want to stop and ask yourself,

"What is the story I am making up here?"

The big idea is to stop. Breathe. Let it land. The new red shiny will still be there. And if it won't be there, then maybe it isn't as red and shiny as you hope. That's the power of the stories we write.

So, if you find yourself feeling stuck, or beat up, or unclear, or out of integrity, or notice that you have lied to protect yourself, or hide, or are confused, or emotionally overwhelmed, or angry, it's a good idea to separate out the facts and then simply own all the stories you are creating.

And own them you must. Because, no one else can own your story. In that sense, your story is inarguable. It might be flat out wrong, based on inaccurate facts, or be clouded by all kinds of long-held beliefs, but it is in truth, your story. No one can take that away from you. And, only you can write a different story. I encourage you to consider doing so.

Question Two In a Nutshell
What is the story you are telling yourself?

- What do you make the data mean?
- What is most significant?
- What "stories" might you make up from this data?
  How does this data affect your view of the future?
- How does this challenge your values and principles?
  Where are you living in a dis-integrated way
  (meaning, your actions are not aligned with your
  values and principles)?
- What long-held beliefs might be in play? What do
  you really think of a person in this situation?
- How are you hiding? Who are you hiding from?
- Are there different perspectives? Is there an
  opposite story that might also be true?
- How might "the other side" view the data?
- What has blocked you from exploring this in the past?
- What can you learn from this? What are the
  implications?

QUESTION THREE:
When you think of that, how do you feel?

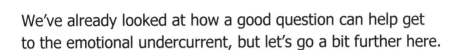

We've already looked at how a good question can help get to the emotional undercurrent, but let's go a bit further here.

Just as I've invited you to separate the FACTS from the FICTION, I am now going to ask you to separate the FICTION from the FEELING. This will allow the story to just be story and to connect to the feelings and sensations that are being generated by the story. When you think about all that:

- What boundary has been crossed? How have you given yourself away? What disappointments have been left un-expressed? You might be feeling **angry**!

- Has something been lost? A relationship? A person? An opportunity? What are you grieving? Who are you feeling sorry for? These all point to the idea of allowing yourself to feel **sad**.

- Is there a bad thing you are trying to avoid? Are you trying to protect yourself? From what? What's the hesitation or resistance about? This is likely good old-fashioned **fear** spinning you in circles.

- And finally, is there something that might be appreciated? A gratitude? A sense of belonging or acceptance? Perhaps some renewal or a "yahoo" moment? And you guessed it... this is what **joy** feels like if you stop long enough to experience it!

So stop! What are you FEELING in your body right now? What does it FEEL like?

George Kinder wrote *"The Seven Stages of Money Maturity"* which is less about money and more about the path to maturity. He coined the phrase, "Let the story go and the feelings be." We use story to generate emotion. Stories create sensations in your body.

Take a moment and reflect on the thoughts came up as you read the previous chapter about the stories you are telling yourself in a specific scene or as you look at your whole life. Think about the critical or dark thoughts you have about yourself. And then stop. Let the story land. Feel.

Breathe.

What are you feeling?

Primary Emotion / Sensations / Feeling Words

SADNESS	Tears, Lump in throat, aching chest	Distraught, Lost, Tender, Down
ANGER	Tense shoulders and neck, clenched and tight jaw, hot head	Angry, Upset, Frustrated, Hurt
FEAR	Fluttering in belly and chest, tension in face, tightness in legs	Afraid, Anxious, Guilty, Worried, Confused
JOY	Bubbling or rushing sensation in chest and down arms, goose bumps, watery eyes	Happy, Grateful, Joyous, Alive, Passionate, Sexy, Excited, Compassionate
ASHAMED OR NUMB	Numbness, general fatigue	Guilty, Embarrassed, Empty, Overwhelmed, Blocked

The big idea with emotion is to experience it! Allow the emotion to flow in and you will discover that it will also flow out. And, be aware of "The rule of not."

When someone tells me what they are "not" there is a very good chance that it is, in fact, exactly what they are. This almost always comes up in conversations around **anger**.

What is it about our polite society that says, "anger is bad?" I'll concede that ramming your car into another car while in a state of rage is bad. But, is all anger bad? Not in my world.

You Have to Feel It!

When you feel angry and you say that you are NOT angry, you are lying to yourself! You are disconnecting from your truth and beginning to create a made-up fantasy story of life as you want it to be. What a waste of energy! When you are mad, it's okay to FEEL MAD!

"I'm not mad. I'm just frustrated." Ha! What's the difference between frustration and anger? NOTHING! Any number of words we use all fall into the primary emotion bucket labeled "Anger" including frustrated, irritated, disappointed, pissed, crossed, de-valued, or violated. These all point to anger. So, kids, when you are angry, express it as anger. "I feel angry!"

AND... keep the baseball bats in the closet. Protect yourself and your loved ones from leaking anger. Go hit a tree. Talk it out with a trusted friend. Go to the batting cages. Try and push that brick wall three feet south. Anything to release some energy so that you can talk about the anger, as opposed to being driven by it.

And, then there is **fear**. I was with a group of colleagues and we were sharing a bit about ourselves.

> *"I get all wrapped up and anxious sometimes when I'm with a group for the first time," I shared.*

"What's the story you make up?" a friend from Canada asked.

"All the usual stuff. I'll suck. They'll hate me. I'll never work again."

"Oh please. Really. What is the picture you are holding?" She could see the question mark on my face. "It sounds like you are holding an outdated picture of yourself."

"Hmm. I suppose that's a possibility. I've worked with hundreds of groups and am still here to tell about it. It's just an ever-present fear for me."

"So, what's the deeper fear?"

"Ha! Good one. Possibly that I'll be damned good. And that might mean I'd have to let go of all this fear baggage I've carried. Argh."

I love the question, **"And, what's the bad thing that might happen?"** It gets you to the risk or fear that might be blocking or gripping you.

The other day, someone asked me the follow up question, **"And, why is that so bad?"**

It stumped me! "Well, because!" was all I could come up with.

Sometimes then, when you can take a step back and reflect for a moment, the bad thing that might happen isn't all that bad.

Fear is tricky. Our mind and our inner world use fear to protect us from harm. I'm grateful for that! And, we want to be conscious of the difference between real fear ("that moose charging me in the forest is real") and made-up fear. Anytime you are predicting a future negative possibility, you are playing with made-up fear. So, get honest with yourself about it. For me, I can see it when I'm sharing my story and I notice myself managing the story, trying to protect myself, because of some made-up possibility of some bad thing that might happen. You might judge me. You might vote me off the island. And again, when I can name the fear and get honest with myself about it I can make a more conscious choice in my next step.

Sadness is kind of a two-sided emotion to me. On one side it is about loss and letting go. And yet, it can also come with a sense of passion, or deep love for something important to me.

One of my deep feelings of sadness came when I got the news one of my old mentors had been killed in a senseless act of violence.

My favorite was a simple turkey sandwich with cream cheese and cranberry sauce at a funky little shop in an old town nearby. Over the course of ten or eleven years that's what I had when Mel and I met for lunch.

Mel owned a machinery business and I loved watching it work. They made small parts for airplanes. I remember he offered math and English classes for his employees which was an unnecessary yet meaningful thing to do back in the day. At lunch we would talk about his business and how it differed from the work I did. He impressed upon me the importance of meeting market demand.

"If you turn someone away you create competition for yourself because someone else will meet the need". Funny the things we remember.

He was a dad and a leader in one of the family programs I managed. As a young buck program director, I remember more than a few enjoyable moments around the campfire. Mel was part of a group of dads who played a subtle yet extremely competitive game of "one-up" when it came to camp cooking. Some of the best steaks and shrimp came off their BBQs accompanied perhaps by a fine glass of Zinfandel. Or two.

Mel took it upon himself to stay in touch with me even after his official role was completed. He reached out and found me at odd intervals, always making it seem like the most natural thing in the world. He showed me a respect that was perhaps not deserved at 25 and 30 years old. Somehow, I always had the sense that Mel "got me." Along with a handful of others, he was instrumental in my early successes not so much by what he did, but how he was. He never took it all too seriously. He held things with a lite grip. He would come with his wife to whatever events we cooked up and was a steadfast supporter.

And, like many mentoring relationships, my time with Mel closed as I moved to a new position in a new city. Life moved on. And, but for a chance meeting at the carwash along the way, I haven't connected with Mel in nearly 20 years. But his presence in my life lived on.

And then I got the news.

A young man on a disconnected rampage took Mel's life. He later took his own life as well. Mel was simply on his way to work early, like always.

And the irony of it is that Mel was the kind of guy that reached out to ensure that young people were known. That young people were connected and welcomed into community. Given respect they didn't deserve. He did it with me. He made it happen for thousands through his support.

When I think of Mel's presence missing, I feel sad. It's a loss. And I also feel passion, love really, for what he brought to the world. He was a guy who cared.

And, pause. Breathe. Allow the sadness to just be.

Where anger tends to live in your body and fear lives in your mind, sadness is something that wants to be allowed in. You can use all kinds of energy to keep sadness out. And, you can choose to allow the wave to come over, the tears to flow. Try it.

Like sadness that wants to be allowed, **joy** seems to be a fleeting emotion that wants to be caught. And, you can miss it if you're not open to experiencing it! One such unexpected moment was the joy that flooded me after my dad died. Joy? How can that be?

I was with my Dad when he stopped breathing. For several hours before, I had been quietly saying to him in his un-responsive place, "Dad, your job here is to breathe. Just breathe. And, you're almost there. You can do it." At 9:15pm he was breathing. At 9:20pm he was not breathing. A few minutes later, two nurses came into his room in the Care Center and declared that he was no longer alive.

I have a belief that there is an invisible realm. We can see neither our "mind" nor our "spirit." They are invisible and non-locatable. So, while my Dad's physical, observable, body was no longer judged to be alive, I make up a story that his invisible parts are very much still alive and well. In my story, my Dad's invisible parts are better off than they have been since he started slipping into dementia years ago. And further, like many people before me who have reported similar experiences, there was the briefest moment in my dad's passing where I believe (and, beliefs are just another story I make up) that the invisible realm became visible to him. I saw it in his eyes. I saw it in the smile that spread across his face like the one that always followed that first bite of the McDonald's ice cream sundaes I used to sneak in for him. "That's gooooooood" he would say in his gravelly voice. He was seeing beyond what I or any of us on this side of the line can see. There was no fear. Only love. And, it was good.

After all the emotions washed over me, it was love in the end. And, joy. A feeling of peace and appreciation for all that my Dad had been in his physical life. I felt joy in his passing, in his freedom from the physical constraints that had held him for so long. I breathed it in, smiled, and felt the sense of belonging and acceptance that comes when all is right with the world. That's joy.

Breathe.

Once the data, thoughts, and feelings have been flushed out, take a moment to get quiet with yourself to let your feelings be. Feel fully. Breathe. Your body needs a moment to experience the sensations generated by your thoughts. So, give your body the moment to just feel. In my opinion, the best sentence structure for expressing emotion has just three words:

"I feel _____ ."

And, the most important part of the sentence is the period at the end. STOP. Let the period land. FEEL!

Question Three in a Nutshell
When you think of that, how do you feel?

- When you think about this issue, what emotions come up?
- What are the adjectives that describe you right now?
- Are you willing to just stop and feel what you are feeling?
- What sensations do you notice in your body?
- What do your tears want to say?
- How is fear of the future or the unknown at play?
- What is the bad thing that might happen? Why is that so bad?
- What costume would your fear want to wear?
- What happens when the fear shows up at the door?
- How is anger or frustration present?
- Have any boundaries been crossed?
- What has been lost?
- What might need to be grieved?
- Your face isn't matching your words. What's really going on?
- If you're not feeling _____, what are you feeling?
- What has been gained?
- What might be celebrated?
- For what are you thankful?
- If you could appreciate one thing, what would it be?
- How is love showing up in this moment?

QUESTION FOUR:

Get clear. What is it you really want?

"Would you tell me, please, which way I ought to go from here?" Alice asked.

"That depends a good deal on where you want to get to," said the Cat.

"I don't much care where--" said Alice.

"Then it doesn't matter which way you go," said the Cat.

"--so long as I get SOMEWHERE," Alice added as an explanation.

"Oh, you're sure to do that," said the Cat, "if you only walk long enough."

Which way should I go? Should I change jobs? Should I end this relationship? Tough decisions are tough! It might be easy to say "figure out where you want to get to first," but it sometimes seems like answering that question is just as hard. Like Lewis Carroll's Alice in Wonderland, we often don't **know** exactly where we want to get to.

What do you do?

How about doing nothing? Put whatever is going on in the pot and let it simmer for a bit.

Doing Nothing is Sometimes The Best Thing To Do.

We talked earlier about the idea of "Doing Nothing Different", but this is a different kind of nothing. This is the "go sit on the beach and stare at the ocean" kind of doing nothing. Navel gazing as it were.

Call it meditation if you want, but just sitting in my "***being***" and "***doing nothing***" didn't come easy to me. It took practice. Still does. I remember a friend I'd chat with now and then on the weekend.

> *"What are you up to today?" I'd ask.*
>
> *"Nothing."*
>
> *"Come on. What does 'nothing' really mean?"*
>
> *"I'm doing nothing. I'm sitting on the couch."*
>
> *"Oh! What game are you watching?"*
>
> *"I'm not watching a game. I'm doing nothing. You might try it sometime."*

Definitely not the way I was wired.

Wallace "J." Nichols wrote "*Blue Mind: The Surprising Science That Shows Being Near, In, On, or Under Water can Make You Happier, Healthier, More Connected, and Better at What You Do.*" He proved with science everything I have believed about being in, on and around water so when I think of "doing nothing" it almost always includes water.

The cover picture on this book is of the deck at a beach house I was a part-owner of for ten years. I would use the house for friends and clients to do personal retreats and often would start them with an hour sitting on the deck alone doing nothing. No conversation. No writing. No reading. Just let the water work its magic. I called this "deck time" and it can happen around any kind of water. If you don't believe me, read J's book. Or, go sit by some water.

My sense is that until the facts, fiction and feelings have been teased apart, the soup will remain in the pot on the stove anyway. Whatever wants you might think you want will be clouded with un-owned stories and un-expressed emotions. So, do the quiet work of unpacking all that while you do nothing. Allow your thoughts to wander. Allow yourself to feel. Allow yourself to beat yourself up for a moment and perhaps shift to simply accepting that you are the kind of person that would be in whatever the chaos is in your life.

But, unless you like mushed carrots, you can't leave the pot on the stove long. Too much simmering in "doing nothing" can turn in to ten years, and then twenty, and then you've got a different set of regrets and emotions to experience.

So, what next?

Go play. Really? Yes, play. When you want to connect with your deepest desires of who you are and what you want in life, go play. Do something creative. Something that is uniquely you. Enjoy yourself. Get dirty. Enjoy being you. You'll be amazed with what happens. And, if nothing happens, at least you will have had some fun.

Play can reveal your deeper wants.

One of my clients shared this about how he took the risk to make playful fun happen despite his crushing schedule, and it helped him find what it was he really wanted.

> *"I just put in my calendar that I was going for a ride. Screw it. If someone wants to complain about me leaving early, let them."*

> *I could sense his passion. But there was a struggle. "What happens when you get out on your mountain bike," I asked.*

> *"Well, I love it! It's challenging! I love the fresh air. It's like I'm a kid again."*

> *"So, what's with the "screw it" part of the story?"*

"Of course, it's the old tape running again that tells me that I am only worthy if I am busting my butt with work.

He smiled as he found himself back in familiar territory. We'd been here before.

"What happens AFTER you take a fun ride on your mountain bike?"

"I feel alive. Healthy. On my game. And, I get a ton of work done. When I've had some fun, my productivity goes off the chart."

"Who in your company would complain about that? It sounds like you've got the old belief around worthiness chiming in even though your life experience suggests you may have a different belief."

"Yes! I do believe that my productivity goes up when I'm feeling healthy. Having some fun is a way of taking care of me so that I can take care those around me."

"And, what is it you are really wanting in your life?"

"I want to be responsible. Productive. Caring."

"Sounds to me like you're getting that."

Playful fun is a way of connecting not only to your joy but also to your deeper desires. And, sometimes it takes some work to get there. I learned this when I decided to take up surfing. This single sport challenged me to bring together learned skills, face risks both real and imagined, lean into the fear, and experience the joy of the moment.

Moving back to California from Colorado gave me a new desire to engage with the ocean. Living a thousand miles from the Pacific had made my heart grow fonder! While I had engaged in other sports on the water, I had always been a bit leery of surfing.

But I was motivated. A former colleague was an excellent surfer and the kind of guy who would have the patience to haul a first-time beginner out into the surf. So, I asked if he'd take me along and he agreed.

Well, at first, I was terrified. "What if I get hurt?" "What if I look stupid?" "What if I don't have what it takes?"

"Are there sharks under me?" "Am I going to cut off that guy and get yelled at?" "Everyone else is a local and I don't know what I'm doing." My mind worked overtime as I paddled and got pounded back by the waves. It took me months to get rid of all the voices in my head. And, it took months to practice and gain the necessary skill to feel even modestly competent. And, eventually I did.

I remember the moment at "The Point" at San Onofre State Beach. A beautifully sunny "San O" day. The surf was gentle with an incredibly long right breaking wave. Along with a few buddies, we paddled out away from the breaking surf and took a few moments to enjoy the moment while straddled on our boards just outside of the breaker. When it was my turn I waited for the right wave and paddled hard to get up to speed. I was up in an instant and could see forever down the wave to my right. My board was aligned perfectly and I was able to stand comfortably in that cool (to me!) easy laid-back longboarding style. It went on and on and I played in the wave.

I PLAYED! The fear had melted away and I played with the wave. It was a like a gentle dance. I pushed, and the wave pushed back. Nothing else in the world mattered at that moment. It was just me and the wave. Bliss! Let all the sharks be damned! I had this!

This all brought me to a place of crystal clarity of how much I enjoy and want adventure in my life. The moment of the uncertain outcome. The fear faced. The engagement with natural wonders. All of it! I want adventure in my life. In fact, it is one of my big life commitments at this point. What about you?

While ***doing nothing*** and ***play*** aren't the only paths to finding some clarity of what you want, they are both nice to try! In my experience, both getting quiet and getting rowdy in playful pursuits opens our hearts. They bring us to the "yahoo!" moments. The simple joy of being alive and present. It gives a glimpse into your deepest essence. The thing that makes your heart jump.

Too often, we are asked, "**What should I do**?" when the better question is "**What do I want**?" or "**What's the desired outcome or future?**" When you are clear on your "want", the "do" part often comes easily.

- What do you really want?
- What is it that you do not have now?
- And if you had that, what would you really have?
- How do your wants align with your bigger purposes?
- Is there a deeper want?
- What might others have to say about this want?
- What else might you want?
- Might you already have what you want? What if you did nothing different?

In my work, I ask questions to help clients get clear on what they want. Here is an example of how that may play out.

> *"I made the commitment a year ago to leave my job. And, today was my last day," he said.*

> *"What was it you wanted that you weren't getting in your job?" I asked.*

"I have wanted to work for myself for twenty years. I have ideas to pursue. It felt like time was just marching by."

"What has kept you from doing this before?"

"Responsibility. It just didn't seem like the responsible thing to do. Now it does. I'm ready for this."

"Never stand in the way of a good man with a plan, I say. Keep me posted. Go make it happen.".

It's a beautiful thing when you get clear on what you want in your life or even on a specific issue. A "clear want" cuts through the noise, all the competing voices in your head, all the millions of other options. In gaining clarity on what you want, you often rule out all kinds of things you know you don't want. It focuses you on the positive direction for your life. I love it!

Stating a want or even asking for what you want, not only brings clarity, it also opens the possibility that you may not get what you want. That's a risk. And, that's the next section.

Question Four in a Nutshell
Get Clear. What is it you really want?

- What is it that you do not have now? And if you had that, what would you really have?
- What solution wants to be born now?
- How do your wants align with your bigger purposes? Is there a deeper want?
- What might others have to say about this want?
- What else might you want?
- What if you had no more wants? What would that mean?
- Might you already have what you want? What if you did nothing different?

GET SPECIFIC: UNPACK IT

Take a minute and unpack a specific issue or area of your life that you are open to exploring. This doesn't need to be the deepest and darkest area of your life, but it should be something meaningful where you notice yourself experiencing some sort of emotion or making up a critical or dark story. The Big Idea here is to get really good at separating the facts, fiction and feelings.

And then, sit with your responses in some quiet way AND get out and do something fun and creative after you've taken a stab at writing it out. See what happens to the clarity of what it is you want as you unpack the issue!

Waking Up: Unpacking A Specific Issue

Honor your care and concern for yourself!	I'm noticing that I am emotionally reacting, and I'd like to take the <u>risk</u> of getting clear with myself about…
What is the recordable data? No judgments or analysis.	The specific <u>facts</u> are…
What are your most critical judgments, opinions, analysis, and beliefs? The dark story you make up about <u>you?</u>	The <u>fictional</u> story I make up about these facts is…
What are your emotions? <u>Angry, Sad, Joyful, Afraid,</u> Also: Ashamed, Guilty, Numb	When I think about this, I <u>feel</u>…
What are your desired outcomes, or what you want to release or let go for yourself (and not just the others involved)?	And, I specifically want…

Check for accuracy. Is there more?

Congratulations! You've made it through the first four questions. So far, you've been aimed at getting clarity on what you want either in a specific issue or in your life. So, if you are getting everything you want in your life, then celebrate and keep it up! Do nothing different.

If not, you might be thinking, "Great! I'm clear on what I want. Let's go do some things to get at it!" And, that might be a good thing to do. But I'm going to ask you to hold off for a minute by asking the question,

"If this is what I want in my life or this issue, why don't I already have it?"

It's a tough one! And, it leads us into the next three questions that will help shift your life.

QUESTION FIVE:
Is there more? (Hint: There is almost always more!)

In my world, there is almost always more. Why?

Because, if there wasn't more, you'd probably already have what it is you think you are wanting right now in your life. Almost always, there is something that holds you back from getting to your wants. And, the fun starts when you are willing to get curious about that.

So, what is this "more"?

More is everything you know about yourself that might be coming into play in this issue or in your life at this moment. It could be:

- Some long-held belief you have about yourself.
- The way you give yourself away. Self-betrayal.
- Your aversion to exposure or vulnerability.
- Addictions and all the ways you numb your feelings to avoid pain and discomfort.
- Protective strategies. The way you lie and hide to protect yourself.

Yikes! Is it getting warm in here?

So, let's look a bit deeper at all the ways "more" can be playing in an issue.

How do you uncover long held (and often false) beliefs?

Along the road of life, we learn things. We feel things. We get hurt. We hear messages and believe them... "You don't really want that..." or "you really aren't good enough for that..." We then learn to do things that appear to avoid the hurt as we seek to get what we want. Then, we learn that we don't always get what we want, and sometimes that turns into not knowing what we want so that we won't be hurt and disappointed if we don't get it.

Phew! That's a mouthful.

My sense is that our thoughts (or beliefs, opinions, judgments) and our feelings over time begin to cloud the circuit, or the path, between clear desire and clean action. So, what we end up with is a confusing mass of false beliefs and unresolved emotions that have been stored up over the years invading the clarity of the present moment. We avoid situations out of fear, we over-react out of past hurts, our short-fused anger bludgeons a loved one over spilt milk, or we delude or medicate ourselves into a Pollyanna sense of perpetual happiness.

The willingness to look at, challenge, question, and consider long held beliefs is critical to living a conscious and committed life. This is the root of curiosity. Are you willing to look at how your long-held beliefs might be at play in this situation? In this issue? In your life?

Need an example?

Consider for a moment your long-held beliefs about politics. Your list might include:

- Politicians are all liars and cheats.
- Politicians are noble servants committed to the public good.
- Political discourse is good for civil society.
- Political discourse is just a bunch of posturing and pontificating.
- Republicans are evil. Democrats look out for everyone, not just the rich.
- Republicans are good, responsible stewards. Democrats just throw more money and create more bureaucracy while creating endless regulations to fix problems.

I remember my parents hosting a party on the night that Barry Goldwater lost the election to Lyndon B. Johnson (Geez, I'm dating myself). Goldwater was the Arizona Republican and Johnson the incumbent Democrat. My parents were Republicans. And guess what? For most of my adult life I voted Republican. I accepted the easy "fiscal conservative, social liberal" belief as the "right way" and frankly never gave it too much thought.

And then my world had a good plate scraping. And I chose to take a more mature look at the kind of governance I believed in. What leadership wanted to look like for me. It was a good journey of inquiry. And, I'm not going to tell you how I vote because the big idea here is the question, "What long held beliefs are you open to questioning?"

Who are the Characters in Your Closet?

Let's go back to the playground of your childhood. Who were the characters? What role did you play? Were you the bully? The mean girl? The shy kid? The athlete? The perky gymnast? The first to use foul language? The gossip? Go there. Be there!

Why? Because it is in those sometimes-difficult moments while you were immature that you learned how to protect yourself. To fit in. To be okay. And guess what? You do the same things today even as a mature adult. When things get hot, uncomfortable, or vulnerable, who do you become?

Here is how it can play out as an adult. This client was sharing a story of how she was not happy about the way she had been reacting to her husband and kids. She was about to discover an old persona from childhood.

"I don't know what happens," she said. "It's like I become someone I don't even know!"

"Who do you become?" I asked with a hint of knowing curiosity.

"A raging bitch! It's like I reach a point and then just lose it. If you're not with me than you're against me. And, if I'm going to have to go it alone, I'd rather just be alone."

"It sounds like you think you're going to end up alone and you make it happen."

"Did I just say that?"

"Well, if we pull apart the pieces. You were feeling frustrated. They weren't with you. You felt alone. And so, Raging Bitch jumped into the driver seat to make it true. Makes sense to me."

"That makes sense? Why would I want to be alone?"

"You tell me," I said with a smile. "When was it safer for you to be alone?"

"Well, of course I know when. When I was a little girl my sisters loved to taunt me. Frankly, I was smarter than the two of them put together, but they were older. They knew how to get me to do everything."

"So, you ended up doing everything. They didn't do their part. So where does the alone part fit in?"

"Well, most days I would just stay away up in my room. Read my books. Build my imaginary worlds. It was safer there. It was better to be away from my sisters. But I didn't like it. It was lonely."

"And, what might have happened if you hadn't done everything they were supposed to do?"

"My older sister was the queen in my dad's eyes. She'd just make an off-hand remark to my Dad and he'd make my life miserable. He'd join in the chorus teasing me. I was happy to stay away from him as well."

"So, in a way, you had a choice. Either be alone and lonely or just jump in and do everything."

"You just described my life today!"

"Well, before we come back to today, let's just appreciate that part of you that jumped in and did more than your share. My guess is that part protected you in those years."

"But it doesn't make as much sense today."

"No, it doesn't. And, that is where you get to pick a new way."

Once she appreciated how she had developed her protective strategy, it was a simple process to let it go and choose a new way of creating the life she wanted.

Most often you protect yourself when you are afraid of getting hurt. It's simple. We've been playing these scripts our whole lives. The man afraid of conflict who "goes small." The woman afraid of being betrayed who turns into an icy cold emotionless villain. The office manager afraid of losing her sense of worth who saves the day by staying until all hours of the night.

I have a few personas I know that I play.

"The Upfront Leader" is a character I learned and played as a teenager. I did it really well. This is how it happened.

> *By the time I got to high school I had written several plays and usually performed one of the lead characters in every school production. I also was the piano accompanist to the school's choir and played in the orchestra. Much of middle school years were spent in the music and drama department.*
>
> *But as a freshman in high school, I began to get uncomfortable. And, when I looked around it seemed like a lot of the kids in drama were different. Especially the juniors and seniors. They dressed different. They kept to themselves. They were cool, but different. My internal radar was warning me that to stay in drama meant that I was going to be*

*different. And, that scared me. I didn't want to be
different.*

*So, I quit drama. I quit piano lessons. And I became
a leader. I got involved in some things where I could
use my skills being in front of a crowd. Because, if I
was in front leading, I could determine how much of
myself to share. I could manage how much of my
story I shared. Or, didn't share. And, it worked for a
long time. When I became uncomfortable with being
too seen, I would just lead. I'd get out in front. I'd
take responsibility for things. And I was good at it.*

I led as a way of protecting myself from being too exposed.
As a young guy fearful that he might be gay, being exposed
was the worst possible thing that could ever happen. So, I
led. If I just stuck to the conventional narrative and did the
right things everything would work out fine, I told myself.

I appreciate my ability to lead. I appreciate the
opportunities it has afforded me. And it has caused me
problems. It has kept me distant from people. Leading
drains my energy and sends me into old tapes of my
younger years.

When I step away from leading from the front, a whole field
of possibility opens including "Facilitator", "Coach",
"Accompanist", "Mentor" and "Friend." Even "Dad" shows
up in a different way when I let down my "Upfront Leader"
persona. In some ways my kids only knew me in this
persona from their younger years.

Today, when I notice myself jumping into a leadership role, it's a great time to take a breath, step back and ask myself:

"What's really going on here?"
"What might happen if I don't lead?"
"How am I trying to protect myself by leading?"
(This last one is usually what stops me in my tracks.)

Not to say that getting out in front and leading the charge isn't a good thing! Sometimes it's exactly the right thing to do. But as my friend Kaley describes it, personas want to be like coats in the closet. You pick the right coat for the day. Not out of neediness or fear, but out of conscious choice.

That's when my inner "*I Must Lead to Protect Myself*" becomes "*I Can Lead When I Choose To*" and my world is often better for it. And, I can always get curious about "How is this 'coat" helping me or hurting me?"

Where are you Trapped By Fear?

Psychologist Kate Ludeman in "*Radical Change, Radical Results*" explores the "Triangle of Fear" and the idea of how, why, and when we all slip into playing the "Villain", "Victim" or "Hero" in our lives.

Which is your favorite?

- The Complainer / The Bad Guy / The Villain

- The Loser / The One to Blame / The Victim
- The Savior / The Cover Up Fixer / The Hero

You might say, "There are a million reasons why doing something else won't work, so why even try?"
Or, "If you people would just get it right, we could keep moving!" Sometimes, you might be unable to see any other options. Whatever is going on is your burden to carry. Or, if you don't save the day then your world will fall apart.

The curious question might be, "Who do you become when things get uncomfortable?"

Kate's big idea is that all three of these "personas" (or characters) actually share a common need to "be right."

- The Villain needs to be right about how wrong you are.
- The Victim needs to be right about how wrong they themselves are.
- The Hero needs to be right because, well, if they're not right then they are wrong and they can't live with themselves.

Radical Change: Radical Results is a good read and helpful to go deeper in understanding the idea of personas that you have learned to take on over a lifetime. You may have all of them!

Sometimes, we can begin to play a character against someone else's character and that's when things can get messy. How do you stop the train? Here's one way.

> *Things were starting to heat up. The couple had been married most of their adult life and knew exactly how to push each other's buttons.*
>
> *'Well, I don't agree with that," he said. "And more, I'm not going to engage. I've thought this through and am confident in my decision."*
>
> *She was visibly upset. "You can't always be right. I'm not always the bad one. I'm afraid of what might happen if we head down that track and don't want to be railroaded!"*

It went on. Back and forth. Sometimes, I refer to this part of the conversation as "*Na Na Na*" followed by the other "*Na Na Na*" and on and on. Escalating stories. Escalating emotions. It's hard to sit through it sometimes. And then she said,

> *"Brits and Dagos!" And, they both laughed.*

Finally! Something was about to shift.

> *"Tell me more," I said with a smile.*
>
> *She explained. "His family has British high society ancestry. Mine is messy-in-the-dirt Italian. When we*

lock horns, he becomes the high-thinking Anglo and I become the explosive and emotional Italian mama."

"So, it's like a safe word?" I asked.

They hadn't thought of it that way. "Well, yes," they both said.

The ability to "pull-up" (a reference to flying a plane and "pulling up" on the nose to avoid crashing) is a step toward curiosity and maturity. It's a way of saying "time out!"

A safe word is a word or phrase that lets everyone (and you) recognize that you are heading down the track of despair and destruction.

Take a breath. Take a step back. Move away from the keyboard. Take that coat off for a moment. Do nothing. And then, see if there is a better coat for the occasion.

Watch your Words

Any time you are living in reaction to the world there is a little bit of victim persona creeping into your life.

When the words "I <u>need</u> to" show up it is often a good time to shift gears.

I think of *needs* as things like food, air, water and shelter. Everything else is a *want*. It's also often a *choice*. So, you can choose to do any number of things while grounded in your mature self. Here is how one client reacted to this.

"But I feel so guilty when I take time for myself. It's like I'm taking something away from my wife and kids."

"So, how is that working for you," I asked.

"It's not!"

"So, what's the risk of making a change, or not making a change?"

"I suppose the risk of me changing is that others won't like me and my life will fall apart. And, if I don't do something, my life will just be more of a drain."

"And the possible benefit?"

"That I'll be happy. That I'll feel good and be more available to my family."

"So, are you willing to take the risk in order to possibly get the benefit?"

"I have to. I need to."

"Well, that's arguable," I said. "What if instead of 'needing to' you simply framed it as 'I choose to?'

*"Interesting. One is kind of a victim's **reaction** to what's going on. The other is a more mature posture in **response** to living the life I want to live. I like it."*

"Well said."

What if you are stuck in The Hero persona?

It is hard to listen without fixing - and that's the "hero problem." And, hero-ing is a tough habit to break! It is hard not to suggest the solution or tell them what they should do. The problem with the hero-problem is that the fix is always temporary. It doesn't really solve the problem. It may make you look good in the moment; you might even feel good and important about your contribution. But, in the end, the hero-solution doesn't stick.

I was having coffee with a friend. Our house had been broken into while on vacation and we lost an ancient TV, a nice Bose system, and a bag of currency from all the countries I have visited. Not a great loss, but still a loss. I was sharing how I felt angry violated, sad, and he was responding:

"You need to get an alarm system."
"And, you should add the stolen currency to the police report."
"Actually, you should just get someone to housesit when you are away."

"You live on a busy street. You should get those lights that turn on automatically."
"You should have left on more lights. I would have left more lights on."

Finally, I noticed what was happening and I said,
"You know, you'd make a lousy coach."

And he stopped, looking a little sheepish.

"Yeah, I'd be mad too," he said trying to take off his Mr. Fix-It Man coat and hear my emotion.

So, it was one thing for him to hear and reflect the emotion that I was expressing. That felt good. But I also noticed that the question I wanted him to ask was **"What's your plan?"** because that would have been a good question! And, it would have invited me to move through the emotion I was expressing and into a forward-looking posture. **"What's next?"** is almost always helpful once the emotion of the moment has dissipated.

Of course I would have said, "I don't know!" because I didn't have a plan. What I want though is to explore my thoughts and fears around home security and to put aside all the voices of others so that I can discover what **I** want. Because that's where my life will be lived!

My Dad used to say "Don't should on me." I guess the old man had something there.

What about Your Coats?

When you notice yourself pulling a coat out of the closet, whether it is one for a nice and cozy victim, the rough and rugged villain or the dashing hero - stop. Take a breath. Ask yourself, "What is really going on here?"

Here are a few I've met in my practice over the years. What characters are in your closet?

- The Raging Bitch: Take them out before they get you!
- Weeping Wilma: Break a tear and manipulate the masses.
- The Commander: Leave no room for anyone else to show up. Always be in charge.
- Eeyore the Doom and Gloom Donkey: Wear a raincoat even when the sun is out.
- The Maiden Martyr: Call on her when no one else will do it!
- Go Small AND Go Home: There's nothing big here. Just little ol' small guy. Just stay in your cave.
- Action Jackson: Whatever happens, just DO SOMETHING!
- The Unappreciated Saviour: Why can't they see how helpful you are?
- The Dominatrix: Clever, sly, sultry, dark, bring them under your spell.
- Surfer Dude: Chill out Bro! Everything is perfect. The universe is awesome.

- Voodoo Zen Master: Light some incense, sit on the
  floor, close your eyes, and maybe everything will go
  away.

Is there a Dark Story About You?

Dark stories are the "You Suck" messages you tell yourself.
These are the critical voices inside your head that keep you
in check by reminding you that you really are pond scum.

Sometimes I put on a dark cape and a sinister face and tell
stories about myself. Dark stories. Evil, manipulative,
predatory, ugly stories. Think of stories Gollum would tell in
the *Lord of The Rings.* Or any of the evil villains in any of
the blockbuster movie franchises. The stories that make
your skin crawl about you. "You're twisted." "You're evil."
"You are a lying, cheating, swindling bastard just out for
yourself," kind of stuff. Sarcastic cuts delivered with surgical
precision.

One way to discover your own dark stories is by paying
attention to what you see **in others.** Think of it like a
movie of your inner world being projected on to someone
else. You know you are projecting anytime you see
something in someone else and it bugs you! That's
projection. This client found that he was not aware of his
own projections:

"Sometimes I feel really bad afterwards," the young executive was sharing. "I don't get mad, I get mean."

"What happens when you get mean?"

"I can take someone down at their knees. Make them feel terrible about themselves."

"What is it you tell them?"

"It's always different, but it's usually just super-critical. Super biting. Like, 'how do you even look yourself in the mirror in the morning?'"

"Do you ever say those things to yourself?"

His face went blank. He stared off. He nodded. And the tears followed. A painful nerve had been struck.

When you turn the projector back on yourself, it is sometimes painful to realize that what you are seeing in them is really something you don't like about yourself. Or a way you are critical of yourself. Or a fear that you are like that person.

I was attending a workshop years ago and the facilitator bugged me. I didn't like the way he framed his responses as "truth" when they were just his opinions. He certainly had subject-matter expertise but the topics were also open to all kinds of interpretations, different experiences, and optional points of view. He was a bit arrogant and full of himself.

And guess what! Sometimes I accuse myself of being arrogant and full of myself! And sometimes, because I am the guy getting paid to teach this stuff, I can present my point of view as truth! Ouch! He was showing me my dark story.

Question Five in a Nutshell
Is There More? (Hint: There is Almost Always More)

- What long-held beliefs are no longer serving you?
- What do you know about yourself that could be creating or contributing to this issue?
- What is your part?
- How are your known dysfunctions in play?
- How are you sabotaging yourself?
- What personas have you noticed yourself playing? (Or, what coats are you wearing?)
- When did you first learn to play that persona?
- How are you becoming someone other than your best self?
- What is the dark story you are telling yourself about you in all of this?
- What is the most critical voice in your head having to say?
- What was happening when you have found yourself here before?

QUESTION SIX:
What will you let go of (or accept)?

It's one thing to identify all the ways you trip yourself up, sabotage yourself, beat yourself up, or play the villain, victim, or hero. It's another thing to move past all that shit.

And this is where the idea of risk, letting go, and acceptance come into play. This is my favorite question because it takes all the thoughts, feelings, and wants, mashes it up with all that you know about yourself (the "more"), and creates an open field of possibility.

- Am I willing to let go of a long held belief?
- Can I appreciate the positive intention of the persona I'm playing and simply accept myself as I am?
- Can I let things get really good?
- Am I willing to let go of the fear and take a risk in order to grow?

So, I know you want to start doing a bunch of stuff to fix or change your life. Doing nothing can be hard. But, these questions are likely the ones that will help you break out of an old pattern and insert a new way of believing and a new way of approaching your life. It's the old definition of insanity, "doing the same things and expecting different results" in play. You do well to do some things differently in order to get different results.

Because, if there wasn't some new ingredient needed, you would have likely gotten what you say you want long ago.

Embrace a New Belief

We've talked about identifying long-held beliefs, but now it's time to let go. Remember, **beliefs** include all those stories about yourself that you've picked up over a lifetime. And sometimes long-held beliefs no longer serve you! Sometimes long-held beliefs about yourself were never true in the first place!

Letting go of a long-held belief is easy. Simply embrace a new belief!

For example, you may carry a belief that "I am no good at setting and staying committed to goals." As you reflect on your life, you might discover that you've likely kept jobs, shown up for work, completed projects, or done any number of things that you set out to do! So, reinforce the optimism of your belief about yourself. "In the past, I have believed that I was no good at keeping to goals. Upon reflection of my life today, I am believing that I have the ability to set goals and stick to them." And then, build your action plan under this new belief!

Begin to list beliefs that you have about yourself and your ability to change and grow. And remember, this list will constantly change and grow!

OLD BELIEF	CURRENT OBSERVATIONS	NEW BELIEF
"I am no good at setting and staying committed to goals."	"I've been steadily employed, gotten promoted, been financially responsible, and purchased the home I want."	"I can set and stick to important goals."
"I must protect myself from exposure by whatever means necessary."	"When vulnerabilities are exposed, greater support, connection, and confidence are the result."	"I can be vulnerable."
"Being gay would be disastrous."	I've been out for ten years and my life is full and rich with meaningful relationships.	"I can be me."

When I became curious about long-held beliefs I wrestled with these and others. For you, some good questions might be:

- How has this belief served you in the past? Take a minute and appreciate that! And then, does it serve you today?
- What is the risk of letting go or shifting this belief?
- How might your life look different under a new belief?

Appreciate the Noble Intention

Let's go back to the idea of Characters (or Coats) in your Closet. Can't you just take those deplorable undesirables to the local Thrift Shop and be done with them? Thankfully, the answer to that is no. Because, every character in your closet brought you some sort of necessary protection or comfort at some point in your life. These characters are a part of you. They just might not be helping much today.

So, instead of beating myself up and getting critical when I notice myself jumping into a leadership role (when I really didn't want to), I can simply appreciate that part of me. "Thanks Upfront Leader Guy. I appreciate you and your intention here to protect me."

Don't tell anyone I told you to talk to yourself, but frankly, it's okay in my world to bring some comfort to a part of yourself that is wanting to do something good. Because when you can get to a place of appreciation, you can re-direct the intention into a different response.

> *"Leader Guy, how might you help me get through this in a more grounded or mature way?"*

Letting go of the way Leader Guy has shown up in the past opens me up to new possibilities in how that part of me might help me today.

Let Go of Your Fix It

In her TED talk " *The Power of Vulnerability*", Brene Brown
says we all look for "Two Beers and a Banana Nut Muffin" to
solve just about any emotional storm we might find
ourselves in.

Things getting heated? Pop a beer and grab a muffin. Or
go spend a couple hours scrolling though social media. Or
stay at work. Or have a cigarette. Or check out with some
porn. Or buy something you don't really need.

You know what "Two Beers and a Banana Nut Muffin" is for
you. Let's just call it your "fix it".

"Fix it" is not the correct label but we'll use it because that's
what you're trying to do when you ___fill in the blank___.

Your fix-it is temporary at best. An inadequate bandage. A
distraction to get to the next uncomfortable moment of
trying not to face the reality of your life or your emotional
soup.

But, if your fix-it is keeping you on the desired path and you
are getting all that you want in life, keep it up! "If it works
for you, keep it!" I say. You've discovered the winning
formula. Do nothing different (and let go of complaining!).

But if the fix-it is just a way of protecting yourself from the
vulnerability required to get what you really want in life,
then you might want to have a look. Get curious. Breathe.

Ask yourself again, "I wonder what's really going on here?"

The unfortunate difference between fix-its and other blocks to getting what you really want in life is that the fix it might just be harmful.   Tobacco kills.   A DUI is a terrible offense. Porn disconnects you from reality.   Any of your fix-its can be toxic, hurtful, or addictive.   And that's serious stuff.

So if your fix-its have risen to an unacceptable level of toxicity to you, are hurtful to yourself or others or somehow just out of control, get help.   Professional help.

Brene' says, "It's not what you do, but why you do it" that wants to be unpacked.   Talk about it with a pro.   Unpack it. You know where the trail of destruction leads.   And, while only you can change the course of your life sometimes it takes a small village to come along with you.

> *"I used to be totally disciplined in everything. I had goals at work. Goals in my golf game. Goals at the gym. And, I hit them."*

I began to understand why his Company referred to him as a "Rising Star."

> *"But then, I got married. And then we had a kid who is now three. My discipline has gone to shit. It's everything I can do to make it through the week and then I drink myself through the weekend. I'm not proud of saying this."*

"I get it. Everything changed. Your life got turned upside down from anything you had known. Promotions. Marriage. Kids. Let's take a breath. Is there more?"

Clearly there was more. But being able to see how his fix-it had come about opened the door for him to choose a different path. Instead of a six-hour golf game, he could do a two-hour mountain bike ride. He could create a workout discipline at home. Bench-press his kid. Limit the amount of alcohol in the house when their friends came over for dinner.

Once a fix-it has been identified and owned, let it go. It may have served you once, but it no longer serves you.

Shift The Dark Story

The beautiful moment when I noticed myself getting bugged by the facilitator who eventually became my friend was when I made the shift and began to see him as a movie of me. I could see what was going on and get curious, even laugh a bit at myself.

And guess what? Laughter is the great healer when it comes to dark stories. When you can see your own foibles, your own silly ways of protecting yourself, the old tapes that you know so well, I invite you to laugh. Not in a sarcastic or judging way but in that sort of knowing chuckle that says,

"Here I am again. Isn't this just a hoot?" And then, appreciate what you are learning and know about yourself today and see if there is a different story, a more generous story, that you might create.

Another great healer to let go of the dark, evil, and accusing stories you create is to **over-own the story.**

Back in the day former Vice-President Al Gore was quoted as saying *"I invented the Internet."* The media grabbed it and was poised to have a field day. That he did not exactly say it was irrelevant. It became an overnight lightening rod to skewer his annoyingly arrogant persona.

The expected move here would have been for Gore to defend himself. To explain that he had been mis-quoted, to apologize for a mis-speak, to back pedal and correct his statement.

But that's not what he did. His response was:

> *"I was pretty tired when I made that comment because I had been up very late the night before inventing the video camera."*

What's brilliant about that? It's the counter-intuitive move. He took the accusation " *You're annoyingly arrogant"* and over-owned it. With no defense, he made fun of his own arrogance. And, it stopped the media in its tracks. He skewered the story.

What accusation are you defending yourself from?
What part of it might you own?
What might be the counter-intuitive move?

When I bring the critical and dark stories I beat myself up with into the light, they lose some of their power. "Oh, it's just me being an arrogant prick again! I wonder what's really going on?" And that gets me to curiosity and wonder.

But, there is a caution flag! You cannot poke fun at someone else's dark story! Don't do it. I promise you it does not end well. When you laugh about someone else's inner critical voice, you actually give power to that voice and guess what, YOU become the voice. So watch out, because the sparks will fly. Poke fun at you and only you.

When it comes to the dark stories we tell ourselves, the importance of the counter-intuitive, opposite story, 180-degree shift in perspective cannot be overstated.

When you are feeling accused (even by yourself!), get curious and consider that there is possibly some truth for you in the accusation. It wouldn't sting if there wasn't! And then, you can own it. You can let yourself (and your audience if there is one) know that the accusation has no sting because it's something you've already dealt with. I use this strategy often.

When I first came out many years ago, I was terrified of anyone making a gay joke or derogatory remark in a work setting. Too many years protecting myself from the gay accusation I suppose. I was unsure of myself and unsure how to respond. Over time, I worked my insecure edge and today it has no power over me. And occasionally, I will toss some stupidly stereotypical comment into the mix:

"If you think that was gay wait until you see the matching napkins and flower arrangements I've brought to go with our brunch."

Because, I've learned that those who are compelled to comment about my sexuality are doing so often from some insecure place in themselves. And that's their stuff. And, that's okay. I'm here to help with that.

Can You Let It Be Good?

Think about a time when you and your significant other had a wonderful weekend away. Plenty of sunshine, good food, and fun sex. And then you came home. And had a fight over something trivial. You were experiencing a fresh and new level of love, but something kicked in on the inside that said, "Don't let things get too good!" Why?

Because it might not be safe. It might be risky. It might expose you to a bigger fall down the road.

In "*The Big Leap*" Gay Hendricks writes about the "Upper Limit Problem." It's a good read and I highly recommend it to anyone looking to be more conscious and grounded in who they are. Simply put, the upper limit problem is about how we sabotage ourselves if things start to get too good. Too much money. Too much love. Too much creativity. It doesn't make sense, but we all have it and we all do it. This is how it worked for my one client.

"My yappy roommate has been having a field day with me."

"You mean, your wife? You don't have a roommate."

"No, my yappy roommate. He lives in my head."

"Ah. Tell me more."

"Every time I move into a creative zone he fires up. 'Who do you think you are being all creative? Everything is fine just as it is. Why do you need to keep creating stuff?' It's quite annoying."

"I wonder what your roommate is protecting you from?"

"Protecting me? He's keeping me from moving forward!"

"Sounds like protection to me. What might happen if you moved forward in creative ways?"

"My life would be better! I'm just not getting this! Why would I try and sabotage that?"

"Now, that's a good question. Why would you try to sabotage yourself?"

Got an Upper Limit Problem? Go read the book. And then see if you can ground yourself in the appreciative moment when you notice something just got better or bigger in your life.

More love? Notice it. Express it. Relish it. Talk about how you might both fall back into old patterns. Update the picture of yourselves! Celebrate the win.

More money? Enjoy it! Breathe in the feeling of accomplishment and success.

More creativity? Allow some joyful awesome sauce to pour over you. Appreciate the moment. Appreciate the new you.

Are you Willing to Take the Risk?

It seems that if I "let go" of something than it should be gone. Done. Behind me. But in practice, I find that is often not the case. Sometimes, I let go of something and then an old script or behavior shows up and I am invited to let go of an old belief or fear again. And again. And, that's okay. I didn't get here in a day and I'm not likely going to get to a new way of living in a day either.

Often, the thing to let go is some fear around risk. When you are afraid that something bad might happen, you will protect yourself. Avoid. Hide. So, it's a good idea to get curious about the risks you are attaching to any desire you aspire to in your life.

So, what are some of the risks for going after what you want?

- You might be exposed as not good enough.
- You might be judged. You might fail.
- You might succeed (What!?!). Success might mean more is expected of you.
- You might outshine those who love you.
- You might discover that there is something inherently wrong about you.
- You might leave your people behind.
- And, the list goes on!

Once you've named the fear around the bad thing that might happen, you can get curious about why that would be so bad! And then, what is the good thing that might happen? From there, you get to pick. Do I let go of my fear and take the risk?

If the answer is no, that's okay. It just means you forfeit your right to complain about not having what you say you want in your life. Remember, doing nothing after assessing the risks and saying "no" is actually a boost of energy because you no longer are using brain cycles thinking about what you think you want. Let it go!

If the answer is yes, then go forth boldly. Enjoy the journey of letting go and becoming a more conscious and committed version of you!

Question Six In a Nutshell

What Will You Let Go Of (or Accept)?

- How does it serve you to be right where you are?
- What might you appreciate about the way you've behaved? How has it served or protected you before?
- What is the bad thing that might happen if you were to do anything different?
- Why would that be so bad?
- What is the risk of inaction? Of doing nothing differently?
- How might you become vulnerable if you changed?
- What are the possible benefits of change?
- How has this belief served you in the past? Does it serve you today?
- What might you let go of as you go after what you want in your life?
- Are you willing to take the risks in order to possibly gain the benefits of doing so?

QUESTION SEVEN:
What are you committed to?

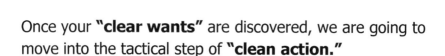

Once your **"clear wants"** are discovered, we are going to move into the tactical step of **"clean action."**

But before taking a bunch of steps forward, it might be good to check in with commitments you have made to yourself and how you choose to live and lead.

You see, I have this crazy belief that whatever results we are getting in life happen to reflect our commitments. And sometimes, those commitments are unconscious. They may not make sense.

This is the bridge between how to get from knowing what you want to knowing what you are going to do. And, it comes down to checking your commitments.

Here's how this played out in one team I was coaching. I was trying to show them how we do things that produce the results we are getting in life.

> *"Silos. Everyone just stays in their silo."*
> *"I can't get a straight answer from anyone!!!"*
> *"All they do is complain and blame some other department!"*

Everyone was moaning.

"Wow. That's some tough stuff," I said. "What would it look like to take 100% responsibility for the results you are getting?"

"These aren't our results!"

They had stepped into my trap.

"Here's what I want you to do. Own these results as something you are committed to." Blank stares. For example, say "I am committed to perpetuating the blaming and complaining."

"What?!?" they cried. "Try it," I said.

Okay, says the VP of Engineering. "I am committed to the blame game." He slumped back into his chair. "I don't like saying that."

"I know," I said.

Let's dig in a bit here.

Once you own some result as that which you are committed to, it becomes conscious. And, that opens the door to the next step which is to get curious about all the ways that you actually do crazy shit that produces the results you are getting. My good friends and colleagues Kaley Klemp (www.kaleyklemp.com) and Delynn Copley (www.delynncopley.com) came up with the idea of creating a "training manual" as a way of owning up to the actions that are producing the undesirable results in your life. Kaley might ask you to "teach me how to be dysfunctional, just like you!" I appreciate their light-hearted approach to what is sometimes serious stuff!

> *"Now, read me a few pages out of the training manual you have written for the blame game."*
>
> *The VP of Engineering grimaced, "Well, you tell everyone that it's the corporate office that wouldn't approve the expense. And then, you be sure the team knows that if marketing had just done their part, we wouldn't be getting blamed. Oh, and forget about offering to collaborate and just simply remind everyone about how busy you are. Okay Vince. I get it. I hate you."*

Sometimes the things we do don't make sense, but when we look deeper, we find that the crazy things we do somehow protect us from vulnerability, criticism, exposure or other unpleasant stuff. So, we do things unconsciously.

The good news is that once we become conscious of it, we can choose a different path. Unless, we'd rather just blame and complain, that is.

Our behavior is the best indicator of our commitments.

You might say that you are committed to getting the results you are getting in your life.   But what if the results are undesirable? Let's walk through this in a bit more detail.

I was facilitating a retreat for executive leaders and things were going okay but the leader of the group had asked me to turn up the heat a bit. No problem.

> *"So, tell me about all the cool things you've been accomplishing in your worlds. Things you've checked off the list, moved the needle on, gotten to the finish line."*

> *The group went around the circle and shared proudly. I jotted some headlines down on the chart pad in front.   "How does it feel to share all that?" I asked.*

> *"Great!" they proclaimed with varying degrees of pride and gratitude. And then, I asked the flipside question, "Tell me about areas where you are stuck or not moving the needle." The collective "argh" was spontaneous because they knew I was up to something. "Come on!" I prodded.*

> *Rick went first.   "My wife and I just aren't on the same page. It's wash-rinse-repeat, tit-for-tat, one upping and all the rest."*

And then Pietro, "My daily schedule is a nightmare. I attend meetings all day every day. I'm late for everything."

Suzanne chimed in next. "I bought a bunch of organizing tools at the beginning of the year and have done nothing. My office is ridiculous. And don't even ask about my inbox. At last count, there were 2,240 unread messages."

And finally Lucy. "I am simply over-committed. I have taken on way too much for one person to handle."

"Thanks. I appreciate your candor. Are you ready to get uncomfortable?"

They groaned.

I was about to show them that The Big Idea with undesirable results is to own the results as something you are committed to. It doesn't make sense because you're unconscious of what you are doing. So, you want to make it conscious and intentional.

"Go ahead and give me the t-shirt version of your unconscious commitment," I chided. And, like the VP of Engineering in the last conversation, they squirmed in their seats.

Rick: "I am committed to a strained relationship with

my wife."

Pietro: "I am committed to being late."

Suzanne: "I am committed to a cluttered office."

Lucy: "I am committed to being over-committed."

"Okay. You're doing great. Now, take it further. How do you DO your Unconscious Commitment?" I asked.

Rick: "Don't communicate plans. Leave the toothpaste cap off. Flirt with others. And a bunch of other stupid stuff."

Pietro: "Never leave a blank space on your Outlook Calendar. Always assume best freeway conditions. Double-book appointments at every opportunity in case someone cancels."

Suzanne: "Keep all files on the desk. Eliminate filing drawers. Never throw anything away!"

Lucy: "Never be alone. Always say yes. Take charge. Never lose control."

"Now we're getting somewhere!"

And again, once you start to own the behaviors that are producing the undesirable result you can get curious about it. You can poke around and look for stories, long-held beliefs, or all sorts of risk aversion tactics that might be in play. Because if there wasn't something going on beneath the surface, you wouldn't be doing these things!

> "*And, how does it serve or protect you to do all that?*"

> "*Okay. You've got to help us with that one,*" they said in unison.

> "*Well, think about it. If it didn't somehow serve you, or protect you from some sort of vulnerability, you wouldn't do it. We're not that complicated. Dig deep.*"

> Rick: "*Okay. I can see how maybe there is a part of me that sometimes believes that if we're always working on the relationship, that the relationship can't end. Keeping up the racket avoids accountability or any kind of an undesirable ending. Am I close?*"

It wasn't quite as solid as I might have hoped for, but he got credit for his curiosity.

> Pietro: "*I feel important. By being late I show that I have power. I can make people wait for me. That sounds awful.*"

Clean. He was getting it.

Suzanne: "By having a cluttered life, I'm the only person who knows where things are. No one else can do my job. I'm in control." She ended with a heavy sigh.

Lucy: "I suppose that by being over-committed I don't have to admit how lonely I really am. Even in a room of people, I feel alone. It feels sad."

"Stay with it, Lucy. What are the tears about? Say more."

"It's just a racket. I know that I over commit. I know that I am not happy with my life. I know that it doesn't make sense. It's just sad."

"Thanks."

While it may seem illogical, behaviors with negative consequences have somehow served you. Because, if they didn't serve you in some way, you would have stopped a long time ago. Connecting to how it serves you creates ownership. It moves you into taking responsibility for all the results in your life. And, until you truly own the unconscious commitment and identify how it serves you, you're stuck.

Once you begin to see how it serves you, you can then assess the risk of behaving in a different way. The risk is often the complement to the "How does it serve you?" question.

"So, what would be the risk for you to change the way you roll? The way you do things?"

Rick: "The relationship might end. I'd be vulnerable."

Pietro: "I might discover that I am not powerful or important enough. I don't like you, Vince."

Suzanne: "If everything was in order I would have to focus on the real challenges and I might fail."

Lucy: "I'd have to face my dissatisfaction."

"You are rocking this. The end is in sight."

And, just as we've talked about before, once you have identified the risks in any situation, it is a simple step to assess your willingness to take the risks in order to possibly get the thing you are wanting in your life.

Next Step: Find a New, Clear and Conscious Commitment

"The next question is a simple one. Are you willing to take these risks in order to possibly get the life you want?"

And, once again, the good news is that a "yes" or a "no" answer are both wins. A clear "no" gives you permission to stop complaining about the results you complain about.

And, a clear "yes" means you have a conscious commitment to work toward with full understanding of the landscape on which to do so.

The idea of risk assessment is common in business. You do it all the time in your life. "Is it worth the risk of getting a traffic ticket or causing an accident to stretch the yellow light that is right in front of me?" You do a quick scan and decide. You do this all day, everyday. And now, you can begin to apply the same risk assessment process in the parts of your life where you are not satisfied with the results. Cool tool!

Assuming you've decided to take the risk associated with getting what you want in this part of your life.

- Give yourself a north star in the sky to guide your steps.
- Frame it in simple, positive language that describes the desired condition. Avoid words like "try", "more" or "better" and instead simply make a firm, positive, intentional statement.

"I am committed to ending stress in my relationship. I am committed to fewer arguments and no flirting."

"Perfect. Except, let's see if there is a way to state all that positively. Give yourself a positive target to aim for."

"How about: I am committed to enjoying the relationship with my wife? Wow. That feels good."

"Exactly. A conscious commitment that moves you toward the life you want will feel good! Pietro?"

"This is easy. I am committed to not being late."

"And if you're not late, what are you? And what about the way you have used your lateness to show power?"

"This is hard! I commit to living my life confident in my relationships and on time. How can I possibly do that?" he exclaimed.

"Let's not worry about the 'how' just yet. Sometimes once we simply make the clear and conscious commitment, the 'how' shows up. Suzanne?"

Well, I won't get this right, but how about, "I am committed to having a clean and organized work space, including my e-mail inbox."

"How does that feel to you?"

"I feel energized saying it. Knowing what it means to me is powerful. I know that I am facing the risks of facing the important stuff."

"Indeed. And, Lucy?"

"I am committed to trying to not do things I don't want to do."

"Uh oh. Here comes the bit about 'trying'..." I trailed off.

"Oh right. I remember Yoda. 'There is no try, only do or do not.' Let's see. This is bigger than just saying yes or no to things."

"Yes, it is! Say more."

"I want to commit to only doing things that are important to me. But more than that, I want to commit to facing the truth of my dissatisfaction with my life."

"Keep going. You're close. And sometimes, it is powerful to simply commit... without the "I want to commit" bit."

"Okay. Here we go. I commit to facing the truth of my life and to ongoing satisfaction."

"Do you believe what you are saying?"

"I do! It feels exciting. Joyful. A little bounce in my step."

More Fuel in the Tank Please

There is beauty and strength in a clear and conscious commitment. So, why not add a little more fuel in the tank to propel you into a new way of living? In a business risk assessment you look at both the risks and the possible benefits. For our purposes here, "benefits" are almost the same as your "wants". And, it's good to connect the two together so that you are crystal clear on the reason for risking vulnerability, failure, exposure, and all the rest!

"Kudos to each of you for making a new commitment. To help you solidify why you are making this commitment and taking these risks, consider for a moment the benefits. What are the benefits to you of keeping this new commitment?"

Suzanne: "I'll feel a sense of ease and focus when entering my office. I'll know what is most important. And I'll save a ton of time not looking for stuff!"

Pietro: "I will be productive AND feel respect for myself. I won't be looking for approval or security from others.""

Rick: "I will have more energy and feel connected to my wife. And, more connected to me, too."

Lucy: "I will be doing things I want to do. I will be honoring my deeper desires."

"Wow. Is it okay if I write about you all in my book? That was solid."

Getting clear on the benefits, or fulfilled wants, of a new commitment provides the motivation and internal drive necessary to stay true to the commitment even when difficult or risky.

Can you predict how you will sabotage yourself?

I was with a company team embarking on a huge redevelopment of their entire software platform. Everyone in the company would be affected. When I held a workshop with them, I told them the story of Shadow Vows.

The night before their marriage, the couple held a ritual where they made their "shadow vows."

The groom said, "I will give you an identity and make the world see you as an extension of myself."

The bride replied, "I will be compliant and sweet, but underneath I will have the real control. If anything goes wrong, I will take your money and your house."

They then drank champagne and laughed heartily at their foibles, knowing that in the course of the marriage, these shadow figures would inevitably come out.

They were ahead of the game because they had recognized the shadow and unmasked it."

I don't know who wrote this, but I love that it's just so blatantly spot-on! Our shadows, our unconscious commitments, our fear-based behaviors... call them what you like... are going to come out.

So, how can you get ahead of the game? This is how it worked in the company context.

My tee up question: "Imagine it's a year from now and you're knee deep in the implementation of your new platform. What are you going to be complaining about?"

The group's response: "Everyone is dragging their feet." "There's no buy-in." "Everyone is keeping their old systems going on the side." "Everyone is blaming us for everything." The team had no problem coming up with this list.

"Okay. So, if these are the results, what is your commitment?"

"We are committed to everyone bitching about the new system!"

After the cheering had calmed down, "Exactly! So, teach me how to ensure everyone bitches about the new software platform."

The group was having fun with this. "Set impossible deadlines!" "Don't communicate changes in the timelines!" "Keep everyone in their silos... never meet as a total team!" "Keep making promises and never deliver!" "Divide and conquer." "Listen but never tell them anything substantive!"

Are you getting it?

Sometimes, you know yourself well enough to be able to predict how you will sabotage yourself. It's an important thing to know.

In my world, I know that when I come in off the road after working a few back-to-back gigs I will be tired. And when I'm tired, I often don't make the best choices about food, drink and rest. I have an unconscious commitment to numb and medicate with multiple "beers and banana nut muffins" when I get home after a work trip. It's an immature response and I know it, and frankly, I give myself permission to go off the rails for a brief time. Bring on the BBQ Potato Chips and Rocky Road Ice Cream!

But now I also have a specific set of practices that kick in on that first day back at home. I do laundry, shop for groceries, connect with a good friend and get a good workout in. I appreciate the moment when I make the shift from Rocky Road to Plain Oatmeal.

So, the good question here might be:

"What can you do to plan ahead for the moments when your unconscious commitments might come online?"

There is one more piece.

It is Okay to Get Help

When an agreement is between you and another person (often, your boss or spouse) – the agreement itself has accountability built in. You are each accountable to your parts of the agreement.

Commitments, on the other hand, are an internal agreement. Absent some agreement with another person on your commitments, you are the only one involved. It is **your** commitment. In that sense, a clear and conscious commitment is an internal north star. It guides your steps and helps you say yes to some things and more importantly, it helps you say no to some things. A clear and conscious commitment is energizing because you use fewer brain cycles to make a choice. You know what you want, you've considered the risks, and you've set the direction for action.

And, it's okay to ask for help! In fact, it's a great idea!

Help for me came in the form of two groups of friends. Both groups met for coffee every Friday morning only in different cities.

Our agreement as a group was to bring an update of what was going on in our lives and how we were living in alignment with our commitments. We made the conscious choice to account for our lives with these trusted few. Nothing was off the table and everything was in a confidential space. There was no fixing or advising, just simply sharing what was important and meaningful with friends we respected and valued.

I simply cannot overstate the value of a small group of peers, committed to walking through the rough and tumble realities of life together. Peer-led groups are common resources for executive leaders. If you don't have one, get one. (And, I can help with that. Check out my book, *"Nine Friends: Maximizing Your Forum"*!).

You can also simply enlist the brainpower of a select and trusted few fellow travelers. I use the "fellow traveler" label as way of saying... "the folks who you know who are also on the road of discovery, self-awareness, conscious living, and all the rest!" A couple good questions for a good friend might be,

"I am now committed to _____.
What advice do you have for me in living by this new commitment?" Or,

"I am committing to a new way of doing _____. Will you help notice when I slip into an old pattern?"

One cautionary note on getting help. People who have a vested interest in your success are often not the best ones to enlist as help. Parents, spouses, kids, and bosses all have an interest in your success. They also have their own fear-based characters, long-held beliefs, upper limits, and more that gets loaded on to any discussion about how you are embracing a new way of living and leading. So, let all those folks see the results and appreciate what they see! Find some others who can walk **with you** but not for you, ahead of you, or behind you.

At this point, you might be wondering, "What is it you are committed to, Vince?' And, that would be a very good question. Because, out of all the good questions to ask, this is the one that puts rubber on the road. Boots on the ground. Actions follow commitment. Even when you are unconscious of it! The truth is, I have a bunch of commitments that have developed over the years since I started waking up. But rather than share a list just yet, let's look at the idea of commitments from a whole life perspective. There is more!

Question Seven In a Nutshell
What Are You Committed To?

- What are the current results in this area of your life? Are you satisfied? Dissatisfied?
- Either way, what do the results in your life suggest you are committed to?
- What are some of the things that you do to produce these results? (Write your Training Manual!)
- How does it serve or protect you to be right where you are? To do what you do?
- What then, might be the risk of embracing a new commitment?
- What might be the possible benefit?
- Are you willing to take the risk?
- What then is a positive commitment or pathway that will move you to the life you are wanting?
- What have you learned about yourself that motivates you to make a new commitment?

THINK BIGGER: COMMITING YOUR WHOLE LIFE

Before we get into the final question and the next steps, I want to elaborate on this idea of making a commitment. Yes, I'm inviting you to do nothing for a bit longer.

Commitments are powerful. They feel good, warm, authentic, and rich. Commitments are full of meaning because you've done the hard work of understanding both the risks and benefits associated with the commitment. But are they big enough?

> "*So in the past you've been committed to playing small. To being uncommitted.*" I was teeing up a question on what he was committed to in his day to day activities and life. "*When we talked last time, you wanted to show up as your true self. To be seen. To bring the best of you. So, as you think about all that now, what is it you want to commit to in this area?*"
>
> "*Well I don't want to be small and uncommitted.*"
>
> "*Okay. If you're not small and uncommitted, what are you?*"
>
> "*Well, duh. The opposite is 'Big,'*" he scoffed. And then "*But that's pretty cliché. Almost arrogant. Who would say that?*"

"Wow. Did you notice what just happened? Whose voice was that?"

"Ha! I just went SMALL as soon as I said the word BIG!"

"Isn't that interesting," I smiled. "What is it you'd really like to commit to?"

"I commit to living the biggest life I can live. To showing up. Bringing it." He breathed. "Damn. That feels good."

Another Big Idea is to look for commitments that encompass your whole life. Not just a part of your life, or the flavor of the moment... but, your whole life. Top to bottom, beginning to end.

To get to commitments that were inclusive of my whole life, I dipped into a deep well of philosophy, spiral dynamics, third force, neuro-science, meta-physics, and all sorts of generally woo-woo hippy-yoga shit. But I won't bore you with all that. I'll keep the big idea in mind. I also invite you to allow these to be points of view, structures, and labels that make sense to me. You may see things differently.

A Simple Line: Be vs. Do

What I see are two fundamental lines of tension within us that begin to make up our internal wiring. We gravitate naturally to different sides of both lines. When our wiring is ignored or misunderstood for ourselves or others, things tend to get complicated. When we begin to understand these two lines, then things get simpler.

On one side of the first line is our need to "do", to act, and produce results. This is where we tend to be focused day to day as we take action and produce results. Folks who live naturally on this side of the line resonate deeply with the Nike slogan "Just do it". In the "Ready-Aim-Fire" command sequence, these folks are "fire-fire-fire."

On the other side of this tension is the need to "be", to understand why and how we are doing what we are doing, or the process. In the fire line command sequence, these folks are "aim-aim-aim," and happy to journal and form learning circles at any time for any topic. They love to remind us that we are human "beings" not human "doings".

BEING  **DOING**

Another way (and arguably a bit more woo woo) is to look at this line as the tension between the visible and the invisible.

Our "doing" is visible. You can see it. An iPhone can record it on video. It is locatable. There is time and space involved. It can be touched.

On the other hand, our "being" is invisible. No one can locate your thoughts. (Really! Check with the neuro science folks! No one has found your "mind"). No one can locate your spirit. Your essence. Your values, beliefs, and purpose are totally and completely invisible. I love Harvard Professor Dan Gilbert's way of putting it:

"The heart goes where the head takes it, and neither cares much for the whereabouts of the feet."

His point is that the invisible parts really don't care much about what the visible parts are up to.

And, for now, I'll just stick with the idea of "being" versus "doing."

Because, the interesting part is the tension that comes in the struggle between the doing and the being. Some folks are wired to be more doing, or action oriented and some are more being, or process, oriented. When "Just Do It" tugs against "Let's Talk About it", someone gets stretched. That's tension.

And, this tension not only exists in relationship. It exists within each of us as well. My values, beliefs, essence, uniqueness, and core purpose get all engaged and mixed up in the simple process of deciding all that I will do today.

Tension is okay. Remember, I'm the guy who is quite comfortable in your discomfort. And tension can be uncomfortable!

When you take a step back and look at your life, to which side of the line do you gravitate? Are you more of a "doer" or more of a "be-er"?

Another Simple Line: "In" or "Out"?

A second line of tension comes from the "how" we go about both being who we are, while also doing what we do. Some of us are wired to focus internally or on ourselves. We think about the task or the problem before us and how we will approach it. Solving problems, staying on task, doing our work in effective and efficient ways all resonate for "results-oriented" people. Folks here respect "problem solvers" and in the command sequence these folks are "ready-aim-fire" and they rarely need to re-load.

On the other side of this second line are those who tend to look outside at all the relationships and other people involved in our lives. Focusing on relationships with both individuals and the group, and all the various and associated human needs all resonate for those who would identify themselves as a "people-person." These are the folks most likely to organize the work softball team or the apres-ski. They are getting "Ready-Ready-Ready" and then take a break.

**SELF/
INTERNAL**

**OTHERS/
EXTERNAL**

And again, how about you? Do you tend to be more internally or self-focused, or more externally or others-focused? There are no right or wrong answers here, just simple self-awareness!

And, my belief is that none of us live on just one point of one of these lines all the time. We're people and we're generally non-linear. So, to try and fit us into a single word box or a point on a line just won't do. Stick with me here, this isn't too complicated- and it will help us get to some deeper understanding of how and why we do what we do.

If we form these two tension lines into a dual axis quadrant, like this,

we can begin to see how the ways we are wired differently as individuals might enrich (or challenge) relationships and serve the greater good of society. It also helps us grab on to the different parts of ourselves. We're all whole people, so any framework that helps us see ourselves through different lenses might be helpful.

Some of us tend to be rooted in caring for our relationships *and* understanding who we are and why we exist. These are the folks who always speak up for our essential purposes, want to look at the long term view, seek diverging opinions, ensure that everyone has had their say and serve on by-laws revision committees. They view themselves as stewards, visionaries, and holders of the sacred and inherent value as an individual, and upon the present day leadership and governance structure by organizational founders. They carry the spirit that gave us life. For identification purposes, we'll call these folks the **"Creators"** for now.

Next, there are those who resonate with getting things done while engaging everyone involved along the way. If it's worth doing it's worth throwing a party for. These are people who see a brighter future and want everyone to come along with them because we'll all be better for it. We'll be changed people. They are strategists and builders. Folks who live here are having way too much fun while they are creating a new world. What they might lack in technical detail they make up for in charisma and energy. We'll call these folks the **Developers**.

The folks wired into the upper right quadrant are battlefield commanders, or **Warriors**. They are willing to suffer necessary casualties because the results demand it! Focused on the identified problem and producing the necessary actions go hand in hand for those who live here. This is the daily grind, the work of most companies, the daily operations. It is what we do. And, I don't remember ever going out for a beer with someone entrenched here.

And finally, there are the folks who stand behind the front line. They are the supply line, the detail folks. They are focused not only on the problem but how it will be solved. They are the bookkeepers who can't go home until all the columns add up. These are the folks who recognize that without money in the bank we have no home, no company, no capacity. A good day is when all the dishes are stacked up neatly, or the file labels are color-coded and cross-indexed for easy access. I love the **Administrators** in my life.

During the safety briefing on any commercial airline, the flight attendants always say, "Put your own oxygen mask on first before helping others." So, put on your own oxygen mask and understand how you're wired. And then, you can begin to see how others around you are wired and how you might connect in meaningful ways.

When my life is in a storm, I do well to look at all that is going on through different lenses. I can look at it from a perspective of any of these characters (or archetypes) to see how I'm doing. To see how my commitments (both conscious and unconscious) are playing out.

Carl Jung was a Swiss psychiatrist and founder of analytical psychology. He was a peer of Sigmund Freud and delved deeply into the idea of archetypes and the collective unconscious. I've given you a book reference in the "Reading and Resources" section later.

Jung believed that we all carry these archetypes within us and can draw upon the wisdom or way of seeing and thinking from these different perspectives. One way I make sense of this is to look at the characters in movies to see how they interact. I'll use a reference here to the *Star Trek* franchise because it both played a part in the formation of my early worldview as a kid and as a franchise has done quite well at remaining culturally relevant. I love the re-boot in the last few years with the new set of actors. So, who are the characters?

Spock: Clearly, Spock represents the administrator archetype. Limited emotional connection but with an ability to synthesize information and produce an unbiased analysis. You know that he is holding the key principles and ideals of Star Fleet Command and takes very seriously his role in protecting the enterprise (and the Enterprise!).

Scotty: The Chief Engineer is our warrior. "I'm giving you all she's got!" he would say. Scotty is never tired. Always loyal. He gets the job done, usually just in the nick of time.

Dr. McCoy/"Bones": While not a perfectly mature representation of the Developer archetype, Bones has a keen sense for "all the bones", or the relationships between everyone on board. He also is deeply connected to the emotional undercurrent and brings that perspective to the team.

Captain Kirk: Like Bones, Kirk is not always the most mature version of the Creator archetype, but he brings the spiritual energy to the team. He is the decision maker. The Executive. He also holds the tension between the other characters, especially the tension between Bones (The Developer) and Spock (the Administrator).

Without any one of these characters, the franchise would not be balanced. In any episode or full-length movie, the resolution of the problem at hand often draws on the resources of all four. Success requires all four characters showing up AND working in alignment. Together, they create a bigger whole.

When we look at these archetypes as "all in all," meaning we all have all these characteristics within us, another Big Idea springs forth! I have one life, I am one person, I am whole, and I am me. And, so are you. The work then is to bring these characters, attributes, and perspectives into alignment. In my world, this is true for a working leadership team and it's also true for you and me.

Let's tease out some different labels that will help you see yourself at a whole-life level and make commitments that support your well-being in each of those areas. You can keep in mind the framework I just shared because it overlays, but this next one is the one I use to frame the commitments in my life.

The Four Squares

So, keeping in mind the idea of the four quadrants framework, let's shift to thinking of it as four squares. Squares imply balance and when our life balances it is a beautiful thing! And, if you look at it from a math standpoint, the four squares together make a bigger square that holds the entirety of your life. So, now we can see how a whole life view might inform your commitments and ultimately lead to the life you want to lead.

I was first introduced to a version of this model by a German speaker at a conference in Dublin, Ireland. The speaker had that lovely German sensibility of unquestionable form and structure and drew on a big whiteboard. Anyone who draws on big whiteboards gets my attention. He also used a bunch of Greek words to back up the structure but I will again work to keep the Big Idea in mind: Our pursuit for a way of living that is clear and conscious.

	INTERNAL/SELF	
THE INVISIBLE: YOUR "BEING"	**Mental Dimension** The part of you that is invisible.	**Physical Dimension** The part of you and your life that is visible.	**THE VISIBLE: YOUR "DOING"**
	Spiritual Dimension Your relationship with all that is outside of you and invisible.	**Social Dimension** Your relationship and actions with all that is outside of you and visible.	
	EXTERNAL/OTHERS	

While this fits into the same four-quadrant framework, the labels are designed to reflect four dimensions of our whole person.

How are you doing so far?

Let's take a closer look at each of the squares and see what there is to be learned.

The Spiritual Dimension: Who are You and Why are You Here?

A few years ago I hiked a cross-country route in the California Eastern High Sierras from Lake George over Mammoth Crest to the Deer Lakes basin and back via Duck Pass. It's about 14 miles from start to finish.

While gathering my gear in the early morning, I pulled out the Ziploc baggie with my maps to find that the one I needed was nowhere to be found. All I had was a map of the entire Forest which had the trails marked but no contour lines. Against my better outdoor judgment, I headed off alone on a cross country route without the correct map.

The hike started on a familiar trail and my mind started to empty out. Thoughts from work and home came and went as I followed the footsteps of the masses. Every now and then, I stop and look up. Check a new view over Horseshoe Lake and the backside of Mammoth Mountain. Look down on Fish Valley and remember a trip of 30 years ago. I'm matching the map in my mind to the mountain before me and it all lines up nicely. I feel a sense of belonging here. I'm at home in these mountains.

The Deer Lakes are a patchwork of interwoven ponds and adjoining creeks. Very quiet and serene on this August morning, but I had the sense of what it could be like on a stormy afternoon when a Sierra Squall had its way. It was new to me. While my family had stories of hiking to these lakes I had never been.

The trail ends at the lakes and the rest of the hike would be off-trail. In my minds map, the route should keep the crest on my left and the lakes on the right but I couldn't quite see how it worked.

There was a steep couloir up to a notch on the left where I thought the trail should be, and a long valley ahead of me which seemed to head away from where I wanted to go. My mind kicked in trying to recapture the view I knew from the other side. I thought I could see hints of trails up the couloir, but could I? I scanned and saw nothing heading up to the other low spot and it seemed too far away, out of place with where I thought Duck Lake should be on the other side. My mind began to get the best of me. Doubt and uncertainty crept in.

I stopped, undressed, and took a dip in the alpine water. It was perfectly bone-chilling snow melt. The kind of water you jump out of as quickly as you jump in. A great little sandy beach was the perfect spot to lay for a half hour or so air drying in the sun and contemplating the situation. I was feeling small in the moment yet also comforted. The mountains have a way of holding me.

Eventually, I needed to take stock. I was alone. No map. Confused about the route. I knew better.

And, as often happens when I take a moment to check in with myself, my mind calms down and fear subsides. I begin to trust in the skills I have. It becomes less about me feeling stupid or wrong, and more about the confidence of being comfortable in my own skin, of remembering that there is something much bigger than me in all of this.

As I pulled on my boots and stood up to head toward the steep couloirs to see if I could find a way, I took a step, looked over the other way to the knoll, and there was a line- the faintest hint of a trail heading up between the two lakes- away from the crest and the nasty couloirs and up the valley to the low spot at the end. I swear that line hadn't been there before.

I gathered my stuff and headed over, feeling a sense of joy at the slightest confirmation of the way I should go. And as often (if not always) is the case in cross country off-trail hiking, the way of the mountain unfolds- but only as I step in. Rarely can we see our path by holding still and scanning. Finding the route requires movement. We move in and it unfolds before us.

As I got to the top of the little gully that formed the pass, the mountain opened up and I stood at the edge of a meadow large enough to hold four soccer fields. You would never know that meadow is there looking up from either side. It's beautiful. And just as that meadow ends, it gives way to another and then glade upon glade as the mountain makes it's way down to Duck Lake. There is no trail, just the occasional rock cairn, strategically placed by those who have traveled this way so that just as you leave sight of one another simply appears where nothing was before. Brilliant.

This is about your relationship to all that is outside of your "self" but that you cannot see. It's about your understanding and sense of belonging in the biggest cultural context, mystery, the divine, of God or however you define your Creator. It's the invisible connection to all living things and your inherent **purpose** for being. It is your "Why?" The spiritual dimension is about your understanding of why you, everyone, and everything is here and expressing gratitude for all of it. And, just as you are "created" you are also "re-created" through fun and playful pursuits that celebrate the joy of simply being alive.

There's that moment when you just feel good in your skin. All is right and you're in alignment with who you were created to be. We'll call this your **Spiritual Dimension** or sense of **Spiritual Well-Being.** I use the label "Dimension" and "Well-Being" almost interchangeably because what I am wanting is to get clear on what creates my sense of well-being across all dimensions of my life.

To me, the spiritual dimension and the desire for spiritual well-being is about:

- Living in appreciation for the beauty of all creation and your part in it. Your sense of belonging.
- **Reflection**, meditation, and prayer.
- Wonder: contemplating the mystery and bigness of the universe.
- Uniqueness: the **treasure** inherent in your individual you-ness.
- How you experience **joy** and **recreation.**

So, how does this apply to your commitments to well-being in life?

- **Reflecting Mindfully**: meditation, breathing, prayer and appreciation. Doing nothing.
- **Catching joy**: pausing to appreciate simply being you in your playfulness, healthy competition, or the pleasure of an intimate sexual experience.

- **Embracing creativity**: sensing your essence through art, music, dance, sport or creative cooking.
- **Cultivating a sense of belonging:** marking the milestones of life including birthdays, graduations, weddings, and memorials. It's also about recognizing both that which makes us different and unique along with that which draws us together into a common humanity.
- **Breathing** deep and valuing each breath.

The Mental Dimension: How Do You Roll and What Guides Your Steps?"

All the stories that live in your head, your long-held beliefs, the principles that guide you all encompass what we'll call the **Mental Dimension** and contribute to your sense of **Mental Well-Being.** And, sometimes, what's going on inside can create some difficult issues on the outside and in relationships.

When I came out gay and entered a new relationship, I came to learn just how many longheld beliefs were rattling around in my head and cluttering up my mental well-being. It was not easy!

When my partner and I met we knew that our connection was a "right place at the right time" sort of thing. I had just gotten back from a trip to Australia and was finally ready to consider a love relationship after five years alone. He had given up looking after recently ending a long-term relationship. That's when he almost ran in to me as I crossed the street.

*Roll the tape forward a few years and I've learned that
living with a middle-aged guy isn't exactly a walk in the
park. We can be grumpy, set in our ways, are happy until
we're not, and generally expect the world to revolve
around whatever it is we're focused on at the moment.
Either one of us can flip from "my way or the highway" to
"just take care of me" in a nano-second. There's a part of
me that believes that just as teens should be shipped off
for the middle-school years, middle-aged men should be
locked away for the five-ten years it takes us to come
through the realization that the sun doesn't rise just for us,
that no one cares nearly as much about our faults as we
do, and we're probably not going to be President of the
United States so get over it.*

*This may sound like a rant about my partner, but it's not.
I'm looking in the mirror. I know that the stuff about him
that bugs me most is all stuff that I see in myself when I
de-fog the mirror and look carefully.*

*A lot of beliefs have been challenged these past few
years. A big one honed over a lifetime and very hard for
me to let go of was the belief that relationships are hard,
contentious, and meant to be a struggle. Bologna.
Relationship is just as hard as I make it. When I choose to
be grounded and connected, relationship is a breeze.
Because whatever is going on in him at that moment is
simply what's going on in him.*

*"Isn't it interesting that he is having a storm right now. I
wonder how I might support him in his storm?" When I
am un-balanced, off-center, non-grounded, and
disconnected, whatever is going on in him becomes a
direct attack on me.*

"Can't we just have some peace in this house? Do I have to fix everything? How did I get put in charge of you?" And the tempers fly, until one of us is willing to stop, take a breath, and usually make the wisecrack, "You know, life with me isn't exactly a walk in the park..."

The mental dimension is about the internal wiring that guides your day-to-day activities and behaviors.

Philosopher Ken Wilber calls the mental dimension the most "I" part of you. It's how you roll. It's your fundamental beliefs, values, skills and principles, or the rails that set a boundary between "good" and "not good". The mental dimension is also where you make sense of the world around you. As life happens, it is in your mind that you make up a story as you assess, evaluate, and apply meaning. It's also where fear lives within you. It's about your commitment to life ideals and values.

- Curiosity, learning, and **knowledge** that protects and equips you.
- Beliefs, values, or principles integrated and updated over a lifetime.
- Moral guiderails, virtues, what it means to live in civil society.
- **Talents** you have embraced and cultivated.

Your mental well-being then has a special role in guiding your commitments to action:

- **Making conscious commitments**: Curiosity with all long-held beliefs, committing to 100% responsibility for the results in your life.

- **Willing** to engage with ideas and concepts that are important or challenging.
- **Clarifying** "How We Roll" in all relationships.
- **Seeking** growth, learning, knowledge and new skills.
- **Understanding** the difference between "what has happened" and "what I make what has happened mean."

The Physical Dimension: What Have You Done Lately?'

While it starts with your physical body, the **Physical Dimension** has to do with all of you that is visible and seen. Your a**ctions,** everything you *do,* including attention to physical well-being, the vocational work that you do, your habits and daily rituals, and how you care for your basic needs of safety and security are included here and all play a part in your **physical well-being**. The way you use time and space all fits in here. A big lesson here came at age 13 during my weekly piano lesson.

> *Mrs. Banks was a formidable presence. She was as wide as she was tall and spoke with an accent from somewhere South. I think it was Argentina. And, she was my piano teacher when I was 13. "Tell me about your practice schedule over the last week," she asked.*
>
> *"Well, it was a busy week. I had school and a lot of things going on." I might as well have said "my dog ate my homework."*

She gave me that look. Her glasses came down on her nose and she looked over the top of them.

"You know, we all get the same 24 hours every day. It's how you choose to use them that makes the difference between brilliant success and dismal mediocrity."

Ouch.

The physical dimension includes your environment and the physical world in which you live. It's about how you live out your **mission**. The physical dimension is about:

- Allocation of attention, **time,** and resources.
- The environment you create for home, work, and play.
- Your vocational pursuits, work ethic, and life balance.
- Expression of your emotional experience.

The physical dimension puts all that is "invisible" within you into practice. These are all your commitments to live out your purpose and principles through your activities and actions:

- Maintaining **discipline** around personal habits of **self-care** and well-being.
- Exercising self-control and balancing rest with activity.
- Choosing work that aligns with your best self.
- Attending to where you are out of balance or tolerating less than optimal conditions. Paying attention to **measurable** results.
- Establishing and sticking to clear agreements.

The Social Dimension: "Where is This Train Headed?"

The social dimension is about the entire constellation of relationships and how you bring your whole self to engage in community with others. Think of the difference between sitting and having coffee alone or enjoying a cup with a friend. Two different parts of you are engaged. The social dimension is visible. It is about how we bring our physical presence and mix it up with others in their physical presence.

One of my biggest lessons in how important the relationships we form are and how we act in community came on the mountain. I've spent a fair bit of my life in the outdoors and it is in fact where many of my bigger life lessons have been learned. The outdoors can be scary, joyful, lovely, and challenging all at the same time. Every part of me is engaged and when I get into the mountains with some friends it just adds to the level of engagement and connection.

In mountaineering, it is hard to miss a summit due to altitude sickness, or not eating well, or dehydration, or suffering mishap and injury, or being turned back by weather. And, it's another challenge to get back on the trail to do it again.

I wrote a blogpost about my attempt to summit Mount Whitney in California and how I suffered from altitude sickness the first time and then bad weather on the second attempt. I had to turn back on both occasions. As it turned out, I only mentioned reaching the summit on the third attempt as a passing remark in the post.

I took some heat from my buddy. He felt I had underplayed what had really happened, for all of us.

> *"Vince this story was far bigger than you make it. The three of us knew the risk that any one of us could falter and that the success of the group making the summit could be compromised. Each of us was willing to give up the personal achievement goal for the health and safety of the other two. There was a huge dynamic taking place that day among us..."*

> *"Trying again for the third time when you knew it would be difficult. Overcoming fear when something had already happened twice. Pushing through in a physically painful state but mentally determined to summit. That was the real story.*

> *"Was it worth it? What did it mean to you personally to be there at that survey cap? More than the one line you gave it in your blog."*

He was right. We did it together and grew as a result. There was something happening that was bigger than the three of us.

It is important to do meaningful things with others. To be recognized for your contribution. To bring together all that you've got in pursuit of a greater good. What could be better?

The social dimension then is living and sharing responsibilities in intimate relationships, practicing good stewardship for all that has been entrusted to you, and providing service with others toward the greater good. The social dimension and your **social well-being** is about:

- Connection: the intimate relationships with loved ones, your circle of friends, and the world beyond.
- **Touch:** the way you interact and touch the lives of others.
- Your **vision:** What you are aiming for and your bigger contribution, the legacy you leave.
- How you build "social capital" and the strength of society.
- Your **passion**. The future that you long for and create.

As with the physical dimension, the social dimension is about your actions, but with the added components of "with whom?" and "toward what end?" You are hard-wired to connect with others. The social dimension is put into practice through your commitments to:

- **Connecting** in **authentic** relationships. Speaking your courageous truth and allowing yourself to be fully seen with others.
- **Serving** some greater purpose to improve the human condition.
- **Engaging** with people different than you and expanding your world view.

As you embrace holistic well-being, you might recognize that balance and maturity includes all dimensions of life!

```
                  FOCUS ON INTERNAL/SELF
```

Mental Dimension	Physical Dimension
Values. Principles. Talents. Beliefs. Knowledge. Clarifies, challenges, protects.	Use of time. Discipline. Boundaries. Mission. Care. Self-control. Measurable actions.
Spiritual Dimension	**Social Dimension**
Connection to your creator and creativity. Wonder and appreciation. Your Treasure. Recreation, reflection, and renewal. Aligns with purpose.	Relationships. Touch. Passion. Connection to others in community and in serving the greater good. Moves toward a vision.

FOCUS ON THE INVISIBLE: YOUR "BEING"

FOCUS ON THE VISIBLE: YOUR "DOING"

```
                  FOCUS ON EXTERNAL/OTHERS
```

A FEW QUESTIONS ABOUT YOUR WHOLE LIFE

Back in Part One, I asked you to take a look at the results you are getting in your life. I promised a deeper exploration at a "whole life" level, and here we are.

Use these questions as thought provokers. Pick one (maybe one that challenges you!) and let it be your "question of the day." Go sit by a lake, take a walk, but be sure to let the questions simmer a bit. There is a worksheet following the questions that you might create (or download at www.vincecorsaro.com) to help you work this through. In my experience, this part of the process can take some time, so be patient with yourself!

Connect to the Spiritual Dimension

- How do you describe your connection to the spiritual? To your most inner being?
- What is it you were created for? What is your purpose?
- When you are all alone and it's just you, what do you enjoy about you?
- What makes you unique? When do you experience your unique creative expression?
- When are you most artistic? Creative? Fun? Adventurous? Playful?
- What are you celebrating? How are you cultivating a sense of belonging for yourself?
- How do you experience joy, gratitude, reflection, and appreciation?

Connect to the Mental Dimension

- How is your mental clarity? When are you most clear?
- What fills your thought life? What do you notice yourself thinking about?
- What beliefs are serving you well? Not serving you? What beliefs may want to be challenged?
- What are the key life principles that guide your steps every day?
- What are you hiding about you? What do you not let the world know?
- How are you experiencing anxiety, making future possibilities real, worrying?

Connect to the Physical Dimension

- What is your sense of self-care? What words describe your relationship with your body?
- How is your home and work environment? What are you tolerating or enjoying?
- Describe your balance of work, rest, eating, and other activities. Are you satisfied?
- How satisfying are the challenges and rewards of daily life?
- Where are your actions aligned or out of alignment with your purpose and beliefs?
- Where do you have crossed-boundaries, injustices, resentments? Where are you giving yourself away?

Connect to the Social Dimension

- How is your connection to the people most important to you?
- Which relationships are working well? Which relationships need some attention?
- Where are you experiencing a sense of community or common cause?
- What is it you are moving toward in your life? What is your vision?
- How are you connected to or serving something bigger than yourself?
- Where are you experiencing loss, grief, or letting go?
- How are you expressing and accepting love in your life?

Getting from Connection to Commitment

It's one thing to become more connected at a whole life level.   The next step then is to focus on becoming more conscious of what you are committed to at a whole life level.

So the question, "What is it I am committed to?" has plenty of meaning.

I know that your life is big and full and can begin to feel way too complex to boil everything down to just a few pithy statements. But guess what? It can be done, using a lot of the questions we've already looked at! Think of it as just a bigger set of binoculars. Or a broader view of your life than just a single issue that is grabbing your attention in this moment. This is how I got from a life that had been thoroughly scraped clean to a set of clear and conscious commitments that have led to a life today that is quite satisfying.

Whole Life Commitment Worksheet

	SPIRITUAL	MENTAL	PHYSICAL	SOCIAL
What are the results you are currently getting in this part of your life?				
What might be your unconscious commitment? What do you do to produce these results?				
How does it serve you to be right where you are?				
What then is the risk for you to change and get a different result?				
Are you willing to take that risk, to possibly get the thing that you want in your life? (Yes/No... and, if "no", stop here and appreciate yourself for setting a solid boundary!)				
Assuming you are willing to take the associated risks, what is your new commitment?				
And, what might be the benefits of staying true to this new commitment?				

QUESTION EIGHT
What is Your Next Step?

So here we are at the last question in the process. You've gotten real about the facts, assessed your stories, and felt your emotions. You've gotten clear on what you want by both doing nothing and getting out to play a bit. You've looked at the risks and benefits and checked those against your bigger commitments.

You might be asking, "Can I just do something now??" You might be frustrated that the carrots in in the pot simmering are turning to mush. So, yes, the answer is yes. You MUST. So, bring it on! But what will you do?

If you've done your work well, action planning is likely the easiest step in the whole game. You know how to create stuff. You know how to take positive action. And you may be learning what it means to take action that aligns with a deeper want and more conscious commitment to who you are and who you want to be.

You really do know what to do.

And, if the actions don't fly, take a breath, step back, and get curious about how it might be serving or protecting you to be right where you are.

Okay Vince, Just Tell Me What To Do!

> *"Vince, how do I ensure that my next steps are the best, most efficient, most productive and most impactful?"*

I hear that question all the time when we get to this point in the process of transition.

And the truth is - I'm not sure. You'll assess that yourself as you evaluate the options and lean into the work. All of us want an easy fix. But there is no such thing.

> *"Frankly Vince, I'd be happy if you just told me what to do here. I'm tired, frustrated, and just want it fixed," she said.*

> *And my 100% guaranteed response when someone asks me to tell them what to do.*

> *"Okay. But first, **what is it you really want?**"*

> *"I already told you I want the situation fixed!"*

> ***"And, if the situation is fixed, what will you have?"***

> *"Well, I'll have peace of mind! I'll know that things are going to be okay! I'll know that I can be the leader I need to be!!!"*

"Ah. So that's what you really want. Peace of mind. Knowing things are going to be okay. Affirming your beliefs as a leader. **Is there more?**"

"Well, I also just want to have a team that I can work with. I want a team that I trust."

"Yeah. I get that. And to have a team that you can trust, **what level of trust do you want in yourself**?"

"Ha! You're tricky. You're suggesting that what I really want is to trust myself."

"Did I say that? It does sound though like that is what you really want, to trust yourself to make good decisions and take appropriate action. **Is that accurate?**"

"Yes. I'm just not sure how to do that in this case."

"Okay. So it sounds like you want to build trust in yourself. So, why don't you ask for advice on how to build trust in yourself to make your own decisions about how to fix your situation. **How does that land for you?**"

"Like work."

"Yep." And, on it goes.

Many of us just want someone else to tell us how to fix it. Just tell me what button to push and I'll push it if makes this pain go away. But is that the end of the story? Sadly, no. There are no easy answers, easy way outs, easy solutions. This life growth shit takes energy, resolve, and perseverance. Trial and error.

But I do have some ways that might make it easier to make sense of your next steps. I tend to lump things together as the "one-offs" or things I will do once and be done with them, and then there are ongoing actions that over time will keep me aligned with my commitments and move my life forward.

What Will You Do in an Ongoing Way?

Sometimes I think of action planning as "aligning my daily life to my ongoing commitments." This means that I can define some daily activities that support my sense of wellbeing across various dimensions.

Look at your commitments across the four quadrants and brainstorm the things that you do or could do to support or stay true to these commitments.

Helpful questions might be:

- What might I do in an ongoing way to stay true to my commitments?
- What are the things I do in a day that make me feel most alive and most connected? How do those things align with my newly stated commitments?
- What are the things I do in a day that drain my energy?
- What might I let go of?
- What might I do differently?

The Big Idea is to define actions that align with your commitments and that you believe contribute to your overall sense of wellbeing when you do them.

For example:

I am committed to being a man of curiosity. How might I live that out in a day to day fashion?

o   I can read for learning and pleasure.

o   I can engage in conversations with others who are perhaps different than me and who challenge my way of thinking or interacting with the world.

o   I can take mental breaks. Give myself time to think and process the events of the day. Time to synthesize and prioritize.

And, all of these can be beneficial. The work comes in our willingness to cull, sort, prioritize and ultimately drop many of our trial action plans. What you want to be left with are the most meaningful and impact-full actions that help you stay true to the commitments you have made.

I can hear you crying, "Twelve things a day? Are you serious?" Breathe. It's okay. You won't do everything every day, but you will notice that the more of these you do, the better you feel about yourself at the end of the day.

So, now you get to pick.

THE DAILY DOZEN

Identify 12 strategies that you believe will best contribute to your sense of wellbeing. Track the strategies that you act upon and then assess your overall sense of well-being for the day. Take time to reflect on what you are learning about you!

		DAYS						
AREAS	STRATEGIES	1	2	3	4	5	6	7
MENTAL WELL-BEING								
PHYSICAL WELL-BEING								
SPIRITUAL WELL-BEING								
SOCIAL WELL-BEING								
	NUMBER OF WELL-BEING STRATEGIES ACTED UPON TODAY							
	OVERALL SENSE OF WELL-BEING TODAY (1 LOW AND 10 HIGH)							

I like to force myself to identify no more than three ongoing actions in any of the four dimensions. This helps focus my effort and attention. And, sometimes a single action can check a couple the box in a couple of dimensions. I love mountain bike riding because I get a physical well-being boost from the exercise of climbing and peddling, a sense of spiritual renewal on the downhill run, and often a dose of social well-being-ness when I do it with a friend or two.

You can always modify your action plans given new information about your commitments or what it is that you are committed to. So, don't worry about the concrete drying on this stuff. You can change it as you experience growth, learning, success, and setbacks.

I put seven blank days on the worksheet so you can give yourself some feedback. Perhaps you will see a correlation between the days you do some good things for your well-being and your overall sense of well-being for that day. Really, this isn't rocket science. Did I mention I once coached a rocket scientist?

> *"So, you really are a rocket scientist?"* I was a bit in awe. I'm kind of intrigued by things that are big and go fast.

> *"Yes. But let's not overplay that joke. Rocket science is predictable and controllable. We know the variables, we know the math, we can solve the problem. Rockets don't talk back. They do what we tell them to do. Every time."*

"Isn't that an interesting idea," I said. "If people were like that, I wouldn't have much of a career."

They call this stuff the "social sciences" but really, what is predictable and controllable when people are involved?

One Offs: Agreements are Everything

Another way to look at taking positive action is to consider what needs to be cleaned up. This might include some changes in structure, re-designed systems, or re-confirmed agreements and expectations. I call these "one-offs" because they are the things you do once and then move on.

Clean-ups can also be an action step to take with another person where you are out of integrity, or living outside of an agreement you have made.

Are We in Agreement?

Agreements are between people. So if you are out of alignment on an agreement you have made it is up to you to step forward to make the correction or re-confirm the agreement. Don't have an agreement? Consider making one. Later I am going to show you how to devise a clear agreement. And, that begs the question, "What makes a clear agreement?"

But we all know that when agreements are unclear, shit happens.

When I was in college I lived for a year with five guys in one house on Sydney Street. Four of us had dogs. And, the dogs were not all that well trained.

Late one night, one of the pups left a present (dog shit) in the living room. One by one, each of us four dog owners came out to look.

"Nope, that's not mine, we each said and proceeded to go back to whatever we were doing. Finally, the guy that didn't own a dog cleaned it up.

The next day someone left toast crumbs on the butter. And someone else got pissed. And then the guy who had cleaned up the dog shit the night before jumped in. And, before it was all done someone had been shoved across the room and fists were about to fly. College life!

So if you want to make "shift happen" (ha!) get clear on your agreements and shift from beating yourself or each other up to respectfully and responsibly doing life.

Devise a 'How We Roll' Document

Hector Barbossa (Actor Geoffrey Rush in "*Pirates of the Caribbean*") said it well, *"The pirate code is really more what you'd call 'guidelines' than actual rules."*

Here is an acronym I learned at a workshop a million years ago called OARRs, as in "get your oars in the water before you start to paddle." I first learned it from a group in San Francisco called Grove Consultants but have also learned variations from others over the years.

Outcomes: Are you clear on the outcomes, or the desired future? What are you aiming toward? What is the desired end state, impact, or difference you hope to create?

Agenda: What will you do? What is the cadence of your activity and conversations? What are the deliverables or action items that you will address? (And, even though that might sound like a business leadership question, it really can apply to any part of your life!)

Rules: This is your "code of conduct" or expected behaviors, your guidelines for respect, timeliness, confidentiality, fidelity (in a relationship), and the like. We can get things done in a civil manner or we can beat the shit out of each other. I prefer civil discourse and constructive conflict. Kaley Klemp wrote a very helpful book called *"The Thirteen Guidelines for Effective Teams"* that really applies to all relationships. She's a pro at this stuff. (www.kaleyklemp.com).

Roles: "Who are you and Who Am I in this?" I like the question "Who is the 'W' and who is the "E" in WE for this issue?" Clear roles help you know whose decision it is, where responsibilities lie, and where accountability will be held.

I lump all these together into what one client calls the **"How We Roll"** Document. I liked the label and use it all the time now. Sounds cool. And, I use these with corporate leadership teams, spouse relationships, families, and to form agreements with myself.

So, if we had these skills during college our **How We Roll** document might have looked like this:

HOW WE ROLL ON SYDNEY STREET

OUTCOMES	Get along. Have fun. Graduate.
AGENDA	Eat together every Monday night. Review the chore sheet and adjust as necessary. Put agreed upon amount in the joint checking account by the last day of the month.
RULES	Keep toast crumbs off the butter. If the owner isn't present, the first one to see a dookie picks it up. Food in the fridge is fair game unless it is marked otherwise. Don't be a jerk. Let others know if you are inviting anyone over.
ROLES	This isn't camp and we don't have a cabin leader. Everyone is responsible for taking care of their own shit. That's why we meet regularly to hold ourselves accountable.

Sometimes just because something is simple doesn't mean it is inadequate, easy, or elementary. Try creating a "How We

Roll" Doc for yourself, your family or your team and see what happens!

Time to Make It Right?

If you have fallen short on an agreement or expectation, it is up to you to offer meaningful apology. Meaningful does not mean you say, "I'm sorry. Let's move on." Meaningful apologies include an honest accounting of your behaviors or transgressions. Apology shows that you are taking responsibility for your actions. And most importantly, meaningful apology comes with the follow up question, "How can I make this right?" Or "How might I repair our relationship?" Without the willingness to make repairs or change behaviors, apology doesn't work. So, making apologies and making it right becomes another possible clean-up step.

Create Structure

Sometimes we need to change some things up. Read a book. Create a new work environment. Buy a gym membership. Find some new friends. And, this is where you can get yourself into all kinds of trouble.

The most common response to dissatisfying results is "doing a bunch of stuff". And, if you've gotten anything out of the last 170 pages, you might decide to focus on doing some things that align with your clear and conscious commitments as opposed to continuing the racket of your unconscious behaviors.

So, with your positive commitments in mind, ask yourself what "structures" might you put in place to support your well-being desires and conscious commitments?

In this sense, a structure is usually a visible or physical thing, like a house. Or a bike. Or a relationship. A structure can also be a regular time allocation or the purchase of a gym membership. A structure could be joining a group of like-interested people. And then, once a structure is in place, you can include the use of that structure into your daily dozen.

"I'd really like to include riding a bike into my daily routine," he said.

"Great! When in your day does riding make sense? Like, is this a mountain bike in the afternoon, or riding to and from work?"

"Oh, I don't own a bike. But, I'd like to ride one."

Seriously? I thought. And, after taking a breath, "Okay. What's your plan then?"

"Well, I'm just thinking this through. I'd like to ride a bike but I'm not sure I want to commit to buying one just yet. But there's a bike shop right around the

corner that rents bikes by the hour. I'll sign up as a customer so I can just pick one up anytime I need it."

"Wow. That was an unexpectedly clear response. It sounds like a solid structure to incorporate into your world."

New Systems = New Ways of Doing Things

In addition to structures you might put in place, there is also room to consider the "systems" you use. Systems are more about "ways of doing things" as opposed to the structures you have put in place.

A system might be the way you organize your food purchases during any week. You may have a system for recording any items you use up, or how you make lists before shopping, or the online services you use for various items. You might also have a financial software system that tracks your income and expenses, helps pay your bills, and keeps track of your deductions or other records. Creating a new system for a way of doing something becomes a one-off clean-up step that again builds into and supports your day to day routine.

In my experience, actions will almost naturally follow your clear and conscious commitments. Someone once said to me, "As soon as you commit to a way of being you begin to become it." I might suggest a corollary could be "As soon as you commit to a way of living you begin to live it."

Question Eight in a Nutshell:
What is your next step?

Ask yourself:
- What is most important, now?
- What's your plan?
- What action will stay true to one or more commitments?
- What are the "one-off" things you can do? How will you know you have completed the task?
- Can you make your action step specific, measurable, achievable, realistic and timely?
- In addition to the one-offs, what might you do in an ongoing way to align with your commitments?
- What behaviors or actions might need to be stopped, started, or continued?
- What systems (or ways of doing specific things) might be enhanced, revamped, re-tooled?
- What structures might be put in place?
- How will you evaluate your actions or know that they were successful?

PART 3

So, you've made it. Here are the eight questions in one handy graphic.

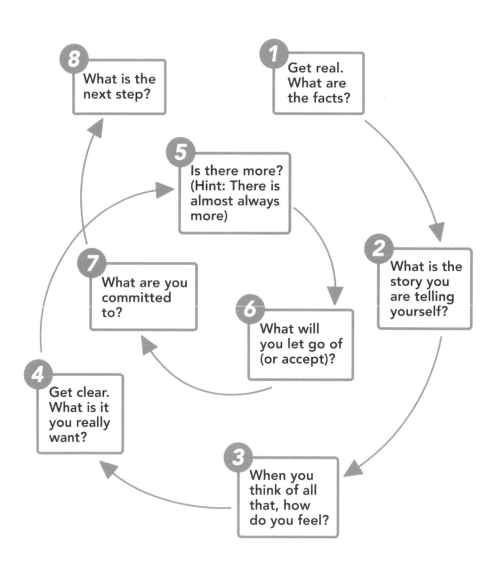

Onward!

While living a committed and conscious life has the potential of bringing you far more joy, ease, and peace, there is no guarantee that life will be easy or free of pain and hardship.

As I write this closing, my life is another f*** mess! My adult kids rarely speak to me. My partner of ten years and I are in a place of ambivalence and disconnection in our relationship. Like many in the United States, I am hooked on the daily news distraction of what our President has said or done today to make life chaotic and unpredictable. I'm worried about the future, my health, and how things are going to play out with my aging mom and siblings.

To celebrate my 60th birthday a few months ago, I skied 63,000 vertical feet in one day with a small group of fellow nut jobs who would do such a thing. Nineteen times down the Beaver Creek Olympic Downhill run "Golden Eagle" plus a dozen other long and fast descents. I was at the top of my game with friends I love. I felt alive, vibrant, strong. The celebratory champagne was sweet.

Two weeks later, I surrendered to "Old Man's Disease" and had my cancerous prostate removed. I had researched all the options but given my young (ha!) age and various risk factors, surgery seemed to be the best option. While the Docs believe I am cancer-free (it will take a few months to validate that), my bladder is behaving like one of our college puppies that peed anywhere, anytime, and my sexual plumbing is completely unhooked. In a moment, my life changed. And, in a world that idolizes youthful vigor (at least, that's the story I tell myself!), I can feel lost, old, and dangerously close to "pasture-ready", as in "time to put ol' Dusty out to pasture."

One of my favorite clients and I amicably parted ways just before my birthday and I miss the creative outlet and close connection I felt with him and his team. Some new companies showed up to grab my attention and I'm curious about how much of myself to invest with them.

There's a cozy coat in my closet that would have me head to the pasture and grow tomatoes in the garden. I'm making up all kinds of stories. Feeling all kinds of emotions.

I wouldn't have it any other way.

And, as I write this, I'm in Sicily, doing nothing, playing often, and sitting with a few good questions.

Instead of another read of Bridges' *"Managing Transitions",* this time I'm reading Chip Conley's "*Wisdom at Work: The Making of a Modern Elder."* It's stirring up ideas and thoughts about navigating into the next chapter of life.

So, if you were hoping to get to this point in the story and have a nice tidy happy ending... well, no such luck! Because, that is the point. Life is messy. It's full of pain, heartache and disappointment. It's also full of adventure, passion, fun, curiosity, and connection. Who would want it any other way?!

When do you feel most alive? Is it when you are resting in unconscious comfort? Or, when life is bringing you some discomfort, challenge, a puzzle to solve or a journey to experience?

Joseph Campbell (the "Hero's Journey" guy. Google him.) wrote, *"People say that what we are all seeking is a meaning for life. I don't think this is what we're really seeking. I think what we're seeking is an experience of being alive."* As for me, alive means playing with all 88 keys on the emotional keyboard and fully experiencing whatever the day brings!

The Big Idea of a committed and conscious life is that, in those moments when you are faced with a choice, you have already thought about what is important to you and what will guide your steps in that choice.

Sometimes you will live in victim-like reaction to what is going on around you and SOMETIMES (not always!), you will respond from a place of maturity and curiosity. Knowing your commitments and being conscious of what is important to you allows you to shift to a place of solid ground. It allows your heart to engage with your mind and to be conscious and fully awake in your next step. So, bring it on.

Onward!

V

Good Questions For Every Question

This is not an exhaustive list, and no one would ever answer every question! Pick your starting point and then scan the questions in that section. Answer the ones that you don't want to answer, or the ones you notice yourself thinking, "Now, that's a good question," or "I don't need to answer that question." If you find yourself claiming certainty about an answer, stop. And get curious with "What might a more curious response be?"

Before You Start

- Have you fully accepted where your life is a f*** mess?
- Where do you see an opportunity for growth?
- What are the risks associated with even looking at your life as it is?
- What long-held beliefs might come into play? What beliefs might want to be put on hold as you explore this?
- Why have you not looked at it before now?
- How does it serve you to not look at your life?
- How might you benefit from looking at your life?
- Are you willing to take the risk of looking in order to possibly gain the benefits of doing so?

Question 1: What are the Facts?

- So, the facts are...
- What has happened? Who? What? When? Where? How Many?
- Is there general agreement on the data by all parties?
- What are three factual bullet points that frame the issue?
- What are the most pertinent and important facts to know in order to assess?
- What could a video camera have recorded?
- What are the verifiable and objective metrics?
- Is there general agreement on the facts?
- What are the differing versions of the facts?
- What would be admissible as evidence in a crime case?
- Where is there disagreement on the facts?
- What are the specific behaviors observed?
- What was the specific time and place?
- What facts are missing? What facts need to be discovered?
- What are your agreements?

Question 2: What's the story you are telling yourself?

- What do you think? What do you make all the facts mean?
- What is most significant?
- What "stories" might you make up from this data? How does this data affect your view of the future?
- How does this challenge your values and principles? Where are you living in a dis-integrated way (meaning, your actions are not aligned with your values and principles)?
- What is the bigger story here? How does today fit into a bigger picture?
- What long-held beliefs might be in play?
- What do you really think of a person in this situation?
- How are you hiding? Who are you hiding from?
- Are there different perspectives? Is there an *opposite story* that might also be as true as this story?
- How might "the other side" view this?
- If it was absolutely safe and confidential to share, what might really be going on? (This is akin to "If I was completely honest...")
- What has blocked you from exploring this in the past?
- What can you learn from this? What are the implications?

Question 3: When you think of that, how do you feel?

- When you think about this issue, what emotions come up?
- What are the adjectives that describe you right now?
- Are you willing to just stop and feel what you are feeling?
- What sensations do you notice in your body?
- What do your tears want to say?
- How is fear of the future or the unknown at play?
- What is the bad thing that might happen? Why is that so bad?
- What costume would your fear want to wear?
- What happens when the fear shows up at the door?
- How is anger or frustration present?
- Have any boundaries been crossed?
- What has been lost?
- What might need to be grieved?
- Your face isn't matching your words. What's really going on?
- If you're not feeling _____, what are you feeling?
- What has been gained?
- What might be celebrated?
- For what are you thankful?
- If you could appreciate one thing, what would it be?
- How is love showing up in this moment?

Question 4: What is it you really want?

- What is it that you do not have now? And if you had that, what would you really have?

- What is the solution wanting to be born now?
- How do your wants align with your bigger purposes? Is there a deeper want?
- What might others have to say about this want?
- What else might you want?
- What if you had no more wants? What would that mean?
- Might you already have what you want? What if you did nothing different?

Question 5: Is there more? (Hint: There is Almost Always more)

- What is your part in creating or sustaining this issue?
- How are your known dysfunctions in play?
- How are you sabotaging yourself?
- What personas have you noticed yourself playing? (Or, what coats are you wearing?)
- When did you first learn to play that persona?
- How are you becoming someone other than your best self?
- What is the dark story about you in all of this?
- Is there a more generous story?
- What is the most critical voice in your head having to say?
- What is the most generous voice in your head having to say?
- What was happening when you have found yourself here before?

- What are the specific things you do to produce these undesirable results?
- Teach me how to be dysfunctional just like you.

Question 6: What Will You Let Go Of (Or Accept)?

- How does it serve you to be right where you are?
- What might you appreciate about the way you've behaved? How has it served or protected you before?
- What is the bad thing that might happen if you were to do anything different?
- Why would that be so bad?
- What is the risk of inaction? Of doing nothing differently?
- How might you become vulnerable if you changed?
- What are the possible benefits of change?
- How has this belief served you in the past? Does it serve you today?
- Which beliefs might be "let go" as you go after what you want in your life?
- Are you willing to take the risk of changing in order to possibly gain the benefits of doing so?

Question 7: What are you committed to?

- What is it you are committed to?
- What is the commitment or pathway that will move you to the life you are wanting?
- What are the risks you are facing in making that commitment?

- What have you been committed to in the past?
- What have you learned about yourself that motivates you to make a new commitment?

Question 8: What's the next step?

- What is most important, now?
- What's your plan?
- What action will stay true to one or more commitments?
- What are the "One-off" things you can do? How will you know you have completed the task?
- Can you make your action step specific, measurable, achievable, realistic and timely?
- In addition to the one-offs, what might you do in an ongoing way to align with your commitments?
- What behaviors or actions might need to be stopped, started, or continued?
- What systems (or ways of doing specific things) might be enhanced, revamped, re-tooled?
- What structures might be put in place?
- How will you evaluate your actions or know that they were successful?

Where to Start When You Are Waking Up

Start by becoming aware, take a breath, decide you want to explore...
and then write your story!

Honor your care and concern for yourself!	I'm noticing that I am emotionally reacting, and I'd like to take the **risk** of getting clear with myself about...
What is the recordable data? No judgments or analysis.	The specific **facts** are...
What are your most critical judgments, opinions, analysis, and beliefs? the dark story you make up about <u>you?</u>	The **fictional** story I make up about these facts is...
What are your emotions? <u>Angry, Sad, Joyful, Afraid,</u> Also: Ashamed, Guilty, Numb	When I think about this, I **feel**...
What are your desired outcomes, or what you want to release or let go for yourself (and not just the others involved)?	And, I specifically want...

Check for Accuracy. Reflect in the second person. (Do this yourself or with an <u>un-involved</u> friend)

Reflect without interpretation. Get to the pertinent data. The "darkest" story. The core emotion. The biggest want.	"So, _____, let me see if I understand you..."
Be silent and check your body. Is this your truth? If not, re-state and reflect again.	"Is that accurate?"

Get Curious! Is there more?

What are your known dysfunctional behaviors, sabotaging patterns, chronic compulsions, protective strategies... that all help create and sustain the issue?	What I know about myself in this is...
How have your behaviors protected you? What are the risks of change? What beliefs no longer serve you?	What risks am I willing to take? What will I let go of?
This is a crucial question. Ask yourself in a kind, genuine, curious way. Work to find your positive and conscious commitment! Destination, not action!	What am I now committed to?

"Clear" does not mean "fixed". "Clear" indicates "heard". Listen to your body. If yes, appreciate yourself!	Am I clear?

Plan your next step. What will you do? Consider any or all:

Clarify Your Commitments and Agreements	*Develop options on resolving the real issue. Make offers and receive counter-offers. Re-confirm your commitments and agreements.* *What might you do irrespective of what anyone else does?*
Apologies and Amends	*Offer meaningful apology to yourself first before others. Generate some self-compassion for being where you are. Ask yourself and then any others, "How can I make it right?"*
Systems, Structure, and Norms Reflection	*What systems (ways of doing things), structures (environments, tools, relationships), or norms (agreements for outcomes, agenda, roles, responsibilities) might you put in place or change for yourself? With others?*

MY PLAYBOOK

This next part is going to unpack my life as I began waking up, in contrast to what I am committed to today. You can skip over all this if you like, and just get to work on your own commitments with the template included with Question #8 and the worksheet on the last few pages. You can also read through to get some of the dirt on me and how I wrestled with longheld beliefs and the risks of change.

I already gave you my current whole life commitments in the opening section, but will remind you here:

Today, my commitment is to be a man of curiosity, with a spirit of adventure and creativity. And, I commit to a life of good self-care and authentic connection with myself and others.

And, to be clear, I'll tie these to the four squares you've just spent 20 pages learning about.

Be a man of curiosity.	Live a life of good self-care.
Embrace a spirit of adventure and creativity.	Connect in authentic relationship with myself and others.

You might be wondering though how all the "unconscious commitment" stuff plays into these clear and conscious commitments. And, that's good! Because, I had plenty of unconscious commitments to explore and understand!

Let me take you on the journey from my life somewhat asleep as an unconscious bystander to a life that is conscious, committed, and continually waking up. I'll start with the "mental" quadrant and go from there.

MENTAL WELL-BEING

The results I was getting: I spent much of my life living in fear of exposure. The results were a defensive posture on almost every aspect of my life. Defensive against my beliefs, my internal wiring, and any sense of integrity. I lived in a constant state of "threat alert" and my internal risk manager was constantly looking three steps down the road to ward off any incoming accusations or revelations.

My unconscious commitment: I was committed to defending and hiding my true self.

How it served me: By hiding my true self, I avoided the shame of exposure as being defective. That God had made a mistake when he crafted me. That I was fundamentally flawed.

The Risks: If I were to not defend and instead show my true self, all my relationships would end. I would be rejected. Judged. I would die a lonely death in a gutter.

The possible benefits: Being true to myself and showing up authentically, being who I was wired to be, would result in an energy gain, a sense of self-acceptance, and a strength that I could only imagine.

Was I willing to take the risks in order to possibly gain the benefits? Yes.

My new Commitment: Being a man of curiosity. What this means to me is that I am in a constant state of "shift" from the defensive posture to the curious. I am open to new learning, new ways of seeing things, new perspectives. I am conscious of my long-held beliefs about everything and am open to curiously exploring whether those beliefs continue to serve me.

What do you think? If you were to take yourself through that line of inquiry, what might you discover? Are you willing to take the risk associated with that?

Shall we continue?

PHYSICAL WELL-BEING

The results I was getting: When I first started this journey of discovery, I lived in constant pain. Injuries had left me with chronic back pain, my hips were out of alignment and my upper body was prone to ongoing pain due to too much swimming and not enough weight-lifting. I lived in a rented condo and had no sense of home base. I was unemployed for the first time in my adult life and had no idea how I was going to provide for my physical needs let alone the needs of my kids as they approached college and adult life.

My unconscious commitment: I was committed to a painful life. (Ouch!)

How it served me: By living in pain, I was able to avoid really embracing what I might want to create. I was reactive. I didn't have to take responsibility for anything because I was "in pain."

The Risks: If I were to live without pain, I would have to take responsibility for where I was at in life. I would have to take the reins and apply myself to the next steps. I would have to risk failure at never having done anything outside of the social sector. There was a risk that I wouldn't have what it takes. I wouldn't have the discipline or strength to get it done.

The possible benefits: Living without pain would eliminate all excuses. I would be free to apply myself. There was the possibility that I might have something to offer the world that would be valued and respected. Instead of blaming or complaining, I could create a world of possibility, freedom, choice, and passion.

Was I willing to take the risks in order to possibly gain the benefits? Yes.

My new Commitment: I am committed to living a life of good self-care. What this means is that I am the owner of this body and that it is my job to take care of it. Period. I am also responsible for the environment I create, whether it is in a rental condo, a home, an airplane or a hotel. I can create a space and a place that is nurturing and free of negative influences. I can also choose the work I do and focus myself in areas that are both good for me and positive to my well-being.

So far so good? Want to keep going? Cool!

SPIRITUAL WELL-BEING

The results I was getting: Yikes. This is hard. I had a very low sense of self. My identity was wrapped up in my work along with the label of "husband" and "dad". The man I knew was more an image than a reality. I was wrapped up in the evangelical Christian framework and had no capacity to look outside that framework for a bigger story or definition of God and creation. I had spent hundreds of hours with therapists and in spiritually oriented classes but all of them had a pre-disposition toward how I was supposed to be over who I truly was. My imperfections were unacceptable to man, God, and me.

My unconscious commitment: I was committed to a life of shame, judgment, and inadequacy.

How it served me: Similar to my unconscious commitments to hiding and pain, living in a place of shame let me never take responsibility for the results of my life. I was the victim. I never had to show myself and could toe the line of other's expectations of who I was supposed to be.

The Risks: If I were to live without shame, I would have to redefine my image of God. I would have to replace all that I had been taught with something that I had been told would lead to certain and immediate death. A life of sin. I would be cast out into the dung heap of unrepentant humanity.

The possible benefits: Perhaps God was truly big enough to hold the bigger story of my life and me. There was a possible benefit of truly accepting myself and all my flaws, with the idea that the inadequacies are that which truly made me unique and valuable.

Was I willing to take the risks in order to possibly gain the benefits? Yes.

My new Commitment: I am committed to a spirit of adventure and creativity. "Adventure" to me is about putting myself into situations where the outcome is uncertain. There is managed risk involved. I can be adventurous in relationships and activities. "Creative" to me is about doing anything off-script. It's keeping a spirit of aliveness and knowing that I am creating and re-creating every day. The world is not happening to me and I am part of a much bigger story. I am creating the results I am getting in life.

And finally,

SOCIAL WELL-BEING

The results I was getting: This is another tough one. The results of a lifetime of a disintegrated identity left me unavailable for authentic relationship. I constructed a life that had limited connection and big walls between the authentic me and the people that others thought they knew. One friend said, "I've known you for 30 years but don't feel like I know you at all." The vision for my life was limited to the impact I could make through my work and had little to do with a vision for intimate relationship, parenthood, or legacy impact.

My unconscious commitment: I was committed to a managed story and to engaging with the world from a place of positive image over authentic truth.

How it served me: Living from a sense of image over substance allowed me to manage the story of me. I could read the crowd and decide what to put forth. My relationships were shallow at best, which meant that no one really knew me. In the shallow place (and in my way of thinking) no one could then judge me inadequate, unworthy, or unacceptable.

The Risks: That I might be judged inadequate, unworthy, and unacceptable by others. That the substance of who I am might not be acceptable to those who I thought I needed in my life.

The possible benefits: Similar to previous conversations, the possible benefits all fall into the category of "an authentic life that is worth living." Letting go of image and the need to manage the story could possibly open the doors to authentic appreciation for the truest me.

Was I willing to take the risks in order to possibly gain the benefits? Yes.

My new Commitment: To connect in authentic relationship with myself, and with others as they connect with themselves. What this means to me is that daily life is a constant exercise in letting go of the man I thought I was supposed to be and embracing the man that I am. And, to live in that way, I am willing to risk rejection, judgment, displeasure, and casting out by others because the benefit of living in authenticity outweighs all those risks.

So, there you have it. These are my commitments today. And, they may change tomorrow as I gather new information, new results, and new perspectives. And, that's okay because commitments are between me and well, me.

The Big Idea of clear and conscious commitments is that they are focused on who you are and who you want to be, given what you know about yourself and your world today. And, all that can change tomorrow. In your maturity, you can always be open to embracing a new point of view or a new position when new information shows up.

But, what is new information? Does a new flavor of ice cream at the market count? Again, a caution flag. It would hardly help if I put my commitments up for assessment every day. That sounds a lot like chasing after the new red shiny we've already talked about. New information to me needs to rise above day to day living. A new job. A new relationship. A new opportunity that couldn't be seen from where I had been standing. New information can also be time-related. After living for a time with my commitment to make my bed every day and know what I wanted for dinner every night it was a natural shift to let that commitment go and move to some higher ground. Make sense?

Now it's your turn. I've shown you mine. Are you willing to take the risk of discovering yours?

To help you out, you can download all the handouts and worksheets at www.vincecorsaro.com.

A LITTLE BIT MORE ABOUT ME

My work today is focused on guiding transformational change for individuals, couples, leadership teams, and peer-led forums. I enjoy working with people who want to work.

As an entrepreneurial leader in the social sector, I spent twenty-five years bringing diverse people together to accomplish significant goals. I have been a successful CEO with hundreds of employees, and on the senior management team looking after 20 million members at 2,500 locations with $4 billion in revenues. Authoring several leadership-oriented resource books has also contributed to my experiences with executive forums and professional associations in North America, Europe, Australia, Africa, and the Middle East.

My time is split between homes in the California desert, the high country of Colorado, and on the Mediterranean Sea in Sicily, Italy. I love most outdoor sports, international travel, a stimulating conversation with a creative meal, and a nice glass of wine at sunset. Let's connect.

More? Check out "The Good Question" at www.vincecorsaro.com or contact me at vince@corsarodevelopment.com for any of these:

- CEO and Executive Leadership Development
- Creating Clarity through Strategic Thinking and Planning
- Resources for Peer-Led Forums
- Forum Training and Retreats
- Coaching and Retreats for individuals, executive and management teams, couples and families.

Reading and Resources

This list is available (and updated regularly) at www.vincecorsaro.com for easy linking.

Resources for small groups:
- Corsaro, Vince. *Nine Friends: Maximizing Your Forum.* Fourth Edition, 2018. (Available at www.amazon.com or for free download at www.vincecorsaro.com).

Articles of Interest (E-mail help@corsarodevelopment.com):
- *Becoming Self-Defined.* An excerpt from *"Toxic Parents: Overcoming Their Hurtful Legacy and Reclaiming Your Life"* by Susan Forward, PhD. 1989.
- *Staying the Course When Things Get Tough.* A narrative and worksheet on clearing issues with self and others.
- *Letting Go and Resetting Life.* An excerpt based on the work of Elizabeth Kubler-Ross, MD.
- *Four Quarter Leadership.* A narrative on the four-quadrant structure from a leadership perspective.

Authenticity, Relationships, and Clear Communication
- Arbinger Institute. *The Anatomy of Peace: Resolving the Heart of Conflict.* 2008.
- Forward, Susan. *Toxic Parents: Overcoming Their Hurtful Legacy and Reclaiming Your Life."* 1989.
- Gottman, John. *The Seven Principles for Making Marriage Work.* 2000.
- Ludeman, Kate, and Eddie Erlandson, *Radical Change, Radical Results.* 2003. (A great introduction to drama, personas, and authentic relationships.)
- Manson, Mark. *The Subtle Art of Not Giving A F*ck. A Counterintuitive Approach to Living a Good Life.* 2016.

Community Building
- Nichols, Wallace J. *Blue Mind: The Surprising Science That Shows Being Near, In, On, or Under Water can Make You Happier, Healthier, More Connected, and Better at What You Do.* 2015.
- Putnam, Robert D. *Bowling Alone: The Collapse and Revival of American Community.* 2000.
- Sievers, Bruce. *Civil Society, Philanthropy, and the Fate of the Commons.* 2010.
- Watters, Ethan. *Urban Tribes: A generation redefines friendship, family, and commitment.* 2002.

Leadership
- Bock, Laszlo. *Work Rules! Insights from Inside Google That Will Transform How You Live and Lead.* 2015.
- Chait, Richard P., William P. Ryan, Barbara E. Taylor. *Governance as Leadership: Reframing the Work of Non-Profit Boards.* 2005.
- Collins, Jim. *Good to Great.* 2001.
- Dethmer, Jim, Diana Chapman, Kaley Warner Klemp. *The 15 Commitments of Conscious Leadership: A new Paradigm for Sustainable Success.* 2014.
- Godin, Seth.
  - *Linchpin: Are You Indispensable?* 2010.
  - *Tribes: We need you to lead us.* 2008.
- Heath, Chip, and Dan Heath. *Switch: How to Change When Change is Hard.* 2010.
- Klemp, Kaley. *Thirteen Guidelines for Effective Teams.* 2010.
- Lencioni, Patrick.
  - *The Advantage.* 2010
  - *Silos, Politics, and Turf Wars.* 2006
  - *The Five Dysfunctions of a Team.* 2002.
- McKeown, Les. *Predictable Success: Getting Your Organization on the Growth Track and Keeping It There.* 2010.
- Sinek, Simon. *Leaders Eat Last: Why Some Teams Pull Together and Other Don't.* 2014.

Personal Growth
- Baker, Dan, PhD. *What Happy People Know: How the New Science of Happiness Can Change your Life for the Better.* 2003.
- Barry, Cliff. The guy has never written a book but is the master at using experiential process facilitation to uncover identities that have been mired in shame and shadow. www.shadowwork.com.
- Bridges, William. *Managing Transitions. Third Edition.* 2009.
- Brown, Brene'.
  - *Dare to Lead. 2018.*
  - *Rising Strong: How the Ability to Reset Transforms the way we Live, Love,, Parent and Lead.* 2017.
  - *The Power of Vulnerability.* 2010 Ted Talk: www.ted.com.
- Conley, Chip. *Wisdom at Work: The Making of the Modern Elder.* 2018.
- Hendricks, Gay. *The Big Leap: Conquer Your Hidden Fear and Take Life to the Next Level.* 2009.
- Kinder, George. *Seven Stages of Money Maturity: Understanding the Spirit and Value of Money in Your Life.* 1999.

- Phillips, Dave. Three Big Questions That Everyone Asks Sooner or Later. 2006.
- Crowley, Chris, and Henry S. Lodge, M.D. *Younger Next Year: Live Strong, Fit, and Sexy until you're 80 and Beyond.* 2007.
- Warner, Jim. "*Aspirations of Greatness*" delves into the four-quadrant leadership model. " *The Drama Free Office* "works with the drama triangle and personas. www.oncourseinternational.com
- Pert, Candace. *Everything you need to know to feel Go(o)d.* 2006.

Sexual Development
- Easton, Dossie, and Janet W. Hardy. *The Ethical Slut: A practical guide to polyamory, open relationships, and Other Adventures.* 2017 (Third Edition).
- Ryan, Christopher and Cacilda Jetha. *Sex at Dawn: How we mate, why we stray, and what it means for modern relationships.* 2010.
- Williams, Walter L. *The Spirit and the Flesh: Sexual Diversity in American Indian Culture.* 1992.
- Ogas, Ogi and Sai Gaddam. *A Billion Wicked Thoughts: What the Internet Tells Us About Sexual Relationships.* 2011.
- Downs, Alan. *The Velvet Rage: Overcoming the Pain of Growing up Gay in a Straight Man's World.* 2012 (Third Edition).
- Venn-Brown, Anthony. *A Life of Unlearning.* 2nd Edition. 2014.

Spiritual Formation/Alternative Orthodoxy
- Bell, Rob. *What is the Bible?* 2017.
- Bourgeault, Cynthia. *The Holy Trinity and the Law of Three: Discovering the Radical Truth at the Heart of Christianity.* 2013.
- Rollins, Peter. *The Divine Magician: The Disappearance of Religion and the Discovery of Faith.* 2015.
- Rohr, Richard. (www.cac.org) *The Divine Dance: 2016. Everything Belongs.* 1999.
- Wilber, Ken. *A Brief History of Everything.* 2nd Edition, 2007. *The Integral Vision.* 2007.
- Wilson, Edward. *Social Conquest of the Earth.* 2012.

Foundational Resources (Older Stuff That's Really Good!)
- Jung, Carl. *The Archetypes and the Collective Unconscious.* 1959.
- Lewis, Clive Staples. *Mere Christianity.* 1952. (And, just about anything else by CS Lewis!).
- Merton, Thomas. *No Man is an Island.* 1955.